BEYOND COERCIVE EDUCATION

BEYOND COERCIVE EDUCATION

A plea for the realisation of the rights of the child in education

Peter Hartkamp

Original title
Het gedwongen onderwijs voorbij
© Peter Hartkamp 2016

Translated and edited by
Peter Hartkamp

Layout
Christel Hartkamp-Bakker

Cover design & illustrations
Liselotte Hartkamp
(The illustration on page 51 is inspired by a cartoon without identifiable rights based on a quote by A. Einstein).

peter@hetgedwongenonderwijsvoorbij.nl
www.beyondcoerciveeducation.eu
www.facebook.com/beyondcoerciveeducation/

Publisher: The Quantum Company
ISBN 978-90-825641-1-2
NUR 840

To Willemijn, Birgit en Liselotte

Contents

FOREWORD

'I WOULD RATHER BE DEAD THAN AT SCHOOL' said our daughter when she was eight years old. She had already indicated that she was not very enthusiastic about school, but never so clearly. In contrast, during the summer holidays, we saw an energetic and curious child, until the last week of the holidays when she became depressed again. This went on until the next summer holidays. When she said she would rather be dead, this was a big wake-up call for us.

Our response was that 'this cannot be the purpose of school'. So we tried to find out what exactly happened at the school that made it so awful. Socially our daughter was doing well. She had many friends and enjoyed herself. It was the schooling itself that was awful. The school did not meet her learning needs in any way. The result was that my partner and I have been working in education continuously since 2000.

Our daughter attended a school where children were relatively free to determine what to do. But those choices appeared to be limited to the order in which she was allowed to do her schoolwork. As it turned out, the choice of what to do did not exist. We spoke to many parents who also experienced problems with schooling. These were parents with children in traditional schools, a Montessori school and a Waldorf school. It struck us that all the problems were the same. Our conclusion was that the problems were not caused by the type of school, but by the school system itself. That was a bit of a difficult conclusion, as outside the state-funded school system there was not much else. At the same time, we as parents were forced by the government to send our children to school.

The only option left, was to set up a school outside the (state-funded) system. This is easier said than done. Firstly, because starting a school is quite difficult and secondly because we both had no experience in education, except from our own school time.

So we started a long search and we looked into concepts such as flow in learning, motivation theories, demand-driven learning and child-centred education. However, with all educational models we encountered, it still remained the adults who ultimately decided what children did. Finally, we discovered the Sudbury Valley School, near Boston. Here, children determine themselves what they do and, in addition, they also control the management of the school, along with the staff members. I still remember the first time I looked at their website. My first reaction was, 'No, that's impossible'. A few weeks later I looked again, then a little longer. Still I was far from convinced. At that time the conditioning of my thinking through my own education proved a severe handicap. Then we ordered a couple of books and started to read; this felt like coming home. An educational model that felt completely right and a school where I would have liked to go myself. The school had already existed since 1968 and there was a large population of former students who did well in life.

So we decided to start a democratic school, De Ruimte, in Soest. In January 2003, we opened and for our three daughters this was the ideal school. When we drove to school on the first day, we came past a small, completely fenced off school square. My daughter said, 'this is a school for battery kids, we are the free range kids'. I think this captures the essence.

By starting our own school the problems of our children were solved, but the problems for us as parents had only just begun!

Our children were revitalised. Headache, abdominal pain and depression disappeared and they developed at phenomenal speed. Just to give a few examples. At her old school, our oldest daughter had only reached level five out of ten of the reading method. After she was freed again, she read a Harry Potter book in two days. There was nothing wrong with her reading abilities, only that the reading method was totally demotivating for her. Our youngest daughters suddenly started to ask questions again. Then I realised that they always questioned everything until they were five. Their curiosity had come back again after four years!

For us as parents the problems started with the first letter of the school attendance officer. The letter stated that we did not meet the requirement of the Compulsory School Act by sending our children to the school we had founded. For us there was much that was unclear about the Compulsory school act as it did not contain any criteria for a school. After the letter of the attendance officer, the school inspectors visited our school. The inspectors found it difficult to assess the school, as they had never seen anything like it. Moreover, the inspectorate had failed to create a regulatory framework for private schools, so they were not really able to inspect the school. Ultimately, the inspectorate did their inspection anyway. They did this because the Minister of Education had promised so in Parliament. That this was legally not possible did not prove to be a problem. The inspection report was negative and then the real problems started for us as parents.

Ultimately criminal prosecution was started against all parents of the school. Because of this enormous pressure on the school many parents and people in the school became scared and the school adapted its pedagogy. The first two parents who were criminally prosecuted were eventually acquitted by the Court of Appeal of breaching the Compulsory School Act, but by then the damage to the school was already done.

We as parents were adamantly against these changes of the pedagogy of the school, as this would result in becoming a traditional school again. Our reason to start the school was that we wanted something completely different for our children.

So we left this school and founded a second school in 2007, The Kampanje in Amersfoort, based on the proven Sudbury model. This school worked very well for our children but the relationship with the government was at an all time low in 2007. The authorities immediately started litigation against us. Because lawsuits progress very slowly in the Netherlands and education is covered both by administrative law and criminal law, the litigation took quite a long time. This was great for our children, as it allowed them to attend a school that they had chosen for themselves. The litigation and trials proved to be pretty tough, as almost everything in the education laws is unclear. This lack of clarity allowed the personal assumptions and beliefs of government officials and judges to become decisive for the outcome of the lawsuits. For our school this proved to be very difficult, as we had established a school based on completely different assumptions and beliefs. The article in the Dutch Constitution 'the provision of education is free' becomes an empty shell if the personal interpretations of government officials determine the freedom of education.

The problem with the personal assumptions and beliefs of government officials was very substantial because these were based on myths. Moreover, children are forced to attend school in the Netherlands. Schools in which the pedagogical freedom is severely limited by the ways in which the education laws are interpreted and applied; what ultimately had made our daughter state that she would rather be dead than at school. This was a fundamental violation of her children's rights, caused by coercion. That's why I use the term coercive education and not compulsory education.

This book is about all of that.

INTRODUCTION: CHILDREN'S RIGHTS AND EDUCATION

Children are so important that the United Nations agreed a special Convention on Human Rights for them; The Convention of the Rights of the Child. With this treaty the signatory governments aim to protect rights like:

- the right to life and to develop (Article 6)
- participation and the right to be heard (Article 12)
- freedom of expression (Article 13)
- freedom of thought, conscience and religion (Article 14)
- freedom of association and assembly (Article 15)
- the right to privacy (Article 16)
- protection against violence (Article 19)
- the right to education (Article 28)
- the right to establish a school (Article 29)
- the right to rest, leisure and play (Article 31)
- protection against economic exploitation (Article 32)
- protection against drugs and psychotropic substances (Article 33)

1

These rights apply to **each individual child** without exception (Article 2). The signatory governments committed themselves to take **all** necessary measures to achieve these rights for **each individual child** (Article 4).

Many of these rights are indeed realised or the governments are committed to do their utmost in order to realise them. With the right to development and the right to education something special is happening. Signatory governments do their utmost to ensure that children are in schools. What happens to the rights of children within the school seems less important. Inside the school many of the children's rights are violated on a large scale. Ten per cent of people remain functionally illiterate, bullying in schools is endemic and the use of psychotropic substances and drugs is substantial, as are violations of privacy. The right to develop to their full potential is only achieved by a few. Additionally the rights of children to leisure, freedom of speech, being heard and freedom of association are severely constrained inside our schools. After all, children are forced to go to school and forced to stay in the school. They must follow the school lessons and curriculum. One possible explanation for the fact that many children's rights are not guaranteed within the schools, could be that schools as we know them are a product of history.

The educational model, as we know it today, was developed in the eighteenth and nineteenth centuries based on the needs of the society of that time. Children's rights were agreed at the end of the twentieth century. However, there seems no explanation why governments failed to achieve children's rights within the schools over the past twenty-five years. Our governments have, by ratifying the Convention committed themselves to take **all necessary measures** to realise children's rights both in law and in practice.

So what makes schools so special that the violations of children's rights could continue for more than twenty-five years? To explore this, the next chapter provides an overview of current educational systems. Next, the history of compulsory education is discussed. How it came into being and how it has been substantially expanded since. Every belief, even the belief that education should be coercive, is based on a number of doctrines or dogmas. In this book a number of these dogmas is disproven in eleven myths. The following chapter explains how the educational system is continuously reinforcing itself. Subsequently, the hangover of more than hundred years of coercive education is shown. It is a short list of large problems created by the current education systems. Next a brief look to the future is provided. The future already exists in many places; the only problem is that the future is not yet available to everyone. The five examples show that different visions of education are possible and can be successful. From these examples I already want to highlight the Democratic schools. Democratic schools are places where the rights of the child are available to the students. In Democratic schools students decide for themselves what they do, when they do it, how they do it and with whom; there is no coercion in learning. Next to this personal freedom in learning, the schools are managed by direct democracy. Students, and staff decide together on matters concerning the school community; the school budget, the school rules and enforcement thereof and hiring of staff and teachers. This might sound very radical, however alumni of the two oldest and well known Democratic schools, Summerhill in the UK, founded in 1921 and the Sudbury Valley school in the USA, founded in 1968, have been very successful. In the last chapter 'the way forward' it is shown what it would take to eliminate the disadvantages of the coercive education system through realising children's rights within all traditional schools.

Despite the many problems of present-day eduction, I remain optimistic about the future. One reason is that mankind has shown phenomenal growth over the last 100,000 years, all free from coercion. All children learn from birth until their fourth year at phenomenal speed. They all learn to walk and talk in order to enlarge their environment and be able to communicate. Not because they are forced in school, but due to their natural drive to learn. It is critically important to allow the natural curiosity of young people, their will and ability to learn, their ability to adapt to their environment to continue after their fourth year and that adults do not to stand in their way. Better protection of children's rights in schools will lead to children who are happier and are better prepared for their future.

COERCIVE EDUCATION, THE LAST TABOO

The term 'coercive education' has been chosen deliberately, while most governments use the term 'compulsory education'. If you indicate that you oppose compulsory education, this is often interpreted as being against learning and development of children, but nothing is less true. Learning and development are very important. So important, that the right to learn and to develop are established in the United Nations Convention on the Rights of the Child. In this book I will show that the coercion in education violates the rights of the child, not only their right to education, but other basic rights as well.

I do realise that most mainstream educators do what they genuinely believe to be in the best interest of the child, but ask them to stand back and think about what school education actually means, especially in light of the lack of input from the student which is now regarded as a human right. Therefor coercive is a fair description.

Children between 5-16 years, and sometimes even 18 years old, are forced to go to school in most countries. Many children do not do this by choice, but because we as a society have arranged it like this. We can therefore say that there is coercion. The effects of this coercion in education are not always positive. In fact there are many negative consequences, which can be read almost daily in the newspapers; illiteracy, school dropout, bullying, stressed-out teachers[1], exposure to violence[2] and widespread use of psychotropic drugs[3] to name a few.

The existing educational systems have many shortcomings; the newspapers are full of them. If you read the comments, the best remedy against the shortcomings of schooling is mostly more schooling: more teaching hours, shorter holidays, more subjects, more tests, more homework, school at an earlier age, further increase of the school leaving age and more pressure to further straitjacket teachers[4].

The coercive education system might be cracking under its own weight, yet there is virtually no one who suggests adjusting or abolishing the system itself[5,6]. People have

---

[1] Central Bureau of Statistics, The Netherlands, CBS 24-11-2014
[2] Kinderrechtenmonitor - 2013
[3] Ritalin Medical mega blunder: www.wijwordenwakker.org
[4] Proposal of Act for professional register of Teachers: www.internetconsultatie.nl
[5] Verbruggen, A. (2007), Discussie met Ad Verbruggen in de Rode Hoed: www.beteronderwijsnederland.nl

differing opinions on many subjects, but virtually all agree that coercive schooling should remain, preferably even more than there is already.

Governments spend more and more money on education. In the past twenty years in the Netherlands the budgets for primary and secondary education have increased by about fifty per cent in real terms (after inflation). However, the results have not increased to the same extent. In fact, the question is whether the results have increased at all. The Social and Cultural Planning Office concluded in its report *Getting value for our tax money?* that 40-50% of children do not reach the government's own standards for education[7]. In a large-scale pilot study with a central maths test in 2012, 60% of secondary school pupils failed the test[8]. About 10% of Dutch adults can be qualified as functionally illiterate (in the USA this is about 14%)[9,10]. Those people can just read their names and maybe the headlines of the newspapers. These are the conclusions of the Dutch government itself about how well the coercive education system is working. The question is how children can best prepare for their future and what kind of education system is needed to

---

[6] Wel, P. Van der, (2014), Onderwijs anno 2025, Kunstzone, thema onderwijs en toekomst, www.rijnconsult.nl

[7] SCP, (2012), Waar voor ons belastinggeld? Prijs en kwaliteit van publieke diensten: www.scp.nl

[8] Middelbare scholieren scoren massaal onvoldoende bij rekentoets (2012) www.nrc.nl

[9] https://en.wikipedia.org/wiki/Functional_illiteracy

[10] Kurvers, J., (2012), Wat weet een analfabeet over taal en schrift?, taalcanon; www.taalcanon.nl

facilitate them.

It is my impression that many parents, children and teachers want the system to be improved, but they are often looking for solutions that are in essence, more of the same: more tests, smaller classes, better teachers and increased funding for schools. The current educational system may have brought many positives in the past but at the moment it seems overstretched. We cannot solve problems by using the same kind of thinking we used when we created them.

The current curriculum-based schooling is the dominant form of education. This is the result of historic developments. Because of this, not only is legislation aimed at this type of education, but also all language and concepts about education. This includes the word education itself.

> CURRENT CURRICULUM-BASED SCHOOLING IS HISTORICALLY GROWN INTO THE DOMINANT FORM OF EDUCATION

When people use the word 'education', they often mean 'schooling'. However 'education' and 'schooling' are not the same concepts. 'Education' can include 'schooling', but education is a much broader concept. As Albert Einstein said: *'Education is what remains after one has forgotten everything one learned in school.'*

Historical development

The foundations of the current compulsory education were developed in Prussia, where they were first used on a large scale in 1794[11]. The Prussian rulers wanted to create a population that could read, write and count, and especially a population that was obedient. There was a great need for obedient soldiers, civil servants and workers. The purpose of the Prussian rulers was to train people for the efficient functioning of their autocracy. The compulsory education for all children was a way to accomplish this. This system consisted of a state curriculum, year groups and state-approved diplomas. The guarantee that only the right teachers instructed children was provided by state certification of teachers[12].

This model is eventually implemented globally and was successful during the industrial revolution. Generation after generation has grown up with this system. There is no scientific basis for this education model; it is a product of a historic development. The indoctrination of the compulsory education system is so effective that most people have come to believe that this is the only way children can learn[13]. This type of education seems to be a new religion.

---

[11] Abbott, J., Ryan, T., (2000), The Unfinished Revolution, Learning, human behaviour, community and political paradox, Network Educational Press Ltd
[12] Prussian_education_system, en.wikipedia.org
[13] Illich, I. (1970), Deschooling Society

Learning under coercion does not work

In this day and age schooling is coercive. Children are forced to go to school and controlled inside school. They have to submit to the teacher, follow the curriculum, complete their homework, do the tests and are required to think in the way school wants them to think. Apart from whether or not government coercion is in an ethical means, there is no evidence that coercion provides the best results. There is evidence however that intrinsic motivation results in more effective learning[14]. The reason often quoted to force children to school is that this is for their own good. But if there is evidence that coercion is not effective or is even counterproductive, does forced schooling not violate the right to education? Does coercion in education not infringe on the rights and freedoms of children, similar to the infringement on the rights and freedoms of slaves and of women in times past?

---

[14] Deci , R.L., Koestner, R.,& Ryan, R.M. (2001), Extrinsic rewards and intrinsic motivation in education: reconsidered once again. Review of Educational Research, 71 (1), 1-27

THE HISTORY OF COMPULSORY EDUCATION

Introduction

Compulsory education was first seen in democratic countries in 1852 in the state of Massachusetts, USA. After fierce debate, compulsory education was introduced for children aged eight to fourteen, for thirteen weeks a year. Many parents were not enthusiastic about this, and at times an armed militia was needed to 'guide' children to school. Over the next fifty years almost all other American states followed. Europe followed a similar pattern. In England compulsory education started in 1880, and in France in 1881, the Netherlands in 1902, and Belgium in 1914. One of the last countries to introduce compulsory education was Spain in 1978. Circumstances differed in the respective countries, but all governments introduced compulsory education to protect children and to suit the needs of the industrialising societies.

Since this introduction much has changed, in the sense that government influence and control over education has become much greater, and that the influence of parents has grown smaller and smaller. Children have experienced change from the protection of their rights, to growing coercion as regards the number of schooldays, school hours, demands of homework and more elaborate and stringent curricula and testing requirements. The next section describes the history of compulsory education in the Netherlands. The Netherlands is often seen as more liberal than many other countries, including in education. Glenn and De Groof (2012) note[15] *'The Dutch can justly claim they have the most pluralistic school system in the world.'* This history is a showcase of how, over a period of more than a hundred years, compulsory education changed from protecting the rights of the child to the coercion of children in schools.

The Netherlands
The history of coercive education started in the Netherlands in 1902, when the Compulsory Education Act was passed by Parliament. The aim was to make it impossible for parents

---

[15] Zoontjes, P.J.J. & Glenn, C.L. (2012) The Netherlands. In: Balancing Freedom, Autonomy and Accountability in Education, Eds. Glenn, C. & Groof, J., Wolf Publishers, Nijmegen. 333-362.

to deprive their children of an education[16]. The intentions of the people drafting this act were laudable: to protect children from negligence and ensure their chance to develop. The Interior Minister explained this as follows in 1899:

> 'The act is based on the rationale that it is necessary to threaten to punish parents who neglect the education of their offspring. That is not an application of a 'system' of state guardianship, but a necessary protection of those who cannot care for themselves'.

Despite the positive intentions of the minister, strong objections surfaced in parliament, against what was seen as state coercion and state education. The minister strongly denied these arguments:

> 'Wrongly it is claimed that the Government objective is not to introduce compulsory education, but compulsion to attend school (...). This view now seems to be based on a misunderstanding. The objective of government is only, as already pointed out by other members, to ensure education for all'.

A review on the origins and history of the Compulsory Education Act shows that these were very fundamental arguments[17]:

---

[16] Tweede Kamer, 1898-1899, Uitleg Minister van binnenlandse zaken H. Goeman Borgesius bij Leerplichtwet 1902, Memorie van Antwoord, Handelingen der Staten-Generaal, Bijlagen.
[17] De Graaf, J.H., (1999), Ontstaan van de Leerplichtwetgeving Van Houten's Kinderwet en de Leerplichtwet 1900: dare.uva.nl

'Opponents of compulsory education feared that too much state activity, of which compulsory education is a demonstration, would lead to 'effeminacy' of the individual citizen. 'She (the State) wants to transfer the natural, God given obligation of the parents to educate their children to the State, and make the parents servants of the will of the State.' (...) The proposal 'withdraws from the parents the right to decide on the mode of education of their children and is based on the principle that children belong to the State rather than to the parents.' This may result in that 'eventually the legislature can not escape from the consequences of the socialist system of state omnipotence, on which this proposed act is based'.

Despite these objections, the Compulsory Education Act was passed in 1902. One may wonder whether this act improved the existing situation. In 1900, two years before the introduction of compulsory education, more than 90% of children already attended school[18]. Other children were home educated. The concerns of members of parliament seemed unjustified. Compulsory education wasn't state education or state coercion. Not in those days.

---

[18] Bakker, N., Noordman, J., (2010), Vijf eeuwen opvoeden in Nederland, p 576, van Gorkum.

From compulsory education to coercive education

The Compulsory Education Acts of 1902 and 1969 were primarily aimed at parents, in order to protect the rights of children to education. This was always done with considerable force. A lower court took away the parental authority of the mother of 'the two sail-boys in 2013[19,20], because her two children were not enrolled in school. That she tried very hard to find a suitable school for her two gifted and dyslexic children, but that all schools refused her sons, apparently did not matter. The Court of Appeal had to step in to reverse this decision. Another example of this heavy handedness involved two parents from the

> THE COMPULSORY EDUCATION ACT, INTENDED TO PROTECT THE RIGHT TO EDUCATION OF CHILDREN, HAS BECOME A MEANS OF PUNISHING WELL INTENTIONED PARENTS

western part of the Netherlands. They were both qualified teachers and spent half a year cycling through Thailand with their children. They had brought schoolbooks and their

---

[19] The 'Sail-Boys' were two brothers who could not find a school that would admit them and who started a campaign in 2013 by sailing around Europe to raise awareness of the fact that students who want to go to school could not go to school.
[20] Zeilmoeder blogt (26-02-2013): www.telegraaf.nl

children received lessons every day from competent teachers. After the holidays, once back in the Netherlands, a judge ruled that they had breached the Compulsory Education Act. The father was jailed for a week. These examples show that the Compulsory Education Act has become a means to punish well-intentioned parents who are conscientiously searching for alternatives.

In addition to the coercion of parents, the Compulsory Education Act is also aimed at the children themselves. Children are now forced to enjoy their right to education! This story of a student shows how this works:

'In 2010 a sixteen year old student decided that school was a waste of time and stayed at home. His parents were not happy about this and tried to persuade him to go to school, but he refused. Next, five policeman showed up beside his bed and took him to the police station. Here he was interrogated for half a day. The police made up a warrant, followed by litigation. The parents had done their best and were not penalised by the court except that they lost their parental authority. The student was sentenced to juvenile prison in order to force him to attend school. A government guardian was appointed to control him.

In the period between the lawsuit and placement in a juvenile prison the student and his parents luckily found a Sudbury school, which he really enjoyed. At this school he continued becoming proficient in ICT. In his last year at school he even set up a business and worked at school on customer assignments. After school he immediately found a job and the company was so happy with his performance that he was awarded a promotion within a few months.'

In a recent study on ensuring the right to education for children who drop out of the school system, the National Children's Ombudsman reported (2013)[21]:

'Over the last hundred years a lot has changed. Over time, learning as a privilege has been replaced by coercive education, which is now valid until the age of eighteen. Compulsory education equals coercive schooling in the Netherlands; parents must ensure that their children are enrolled in school and that they attend this school on a regular basis. From the age of twelve, children are also responsible for regular school attendance.'

So the privilege of children to become educated has transformed over time into coercive schooling for both children and parents. The government uses its monopoly on violence to enforce school attendance.

> **THE RIGHT TO EDUCATION FOR CHILDREN HAS CHANGED TO COERCIVE EDUCATION**

---

[21] Nationale Kinderombudsman, (16 mei 2013), Van Leerplicht naar Leerrecht, Adviesrapport over waarborging van het recht op onderwijs naar aanleiding van het onderzoek naar thuiszitters. Onderzoeksteam mr. drs. J. Stam mr. E.J.M. Vreeburg - Van der Laan BSc.

Limiting home education

The right to home education was such a widely accepted phenomenon in the Netherlands that in 1848 and 1917 parliament did not bother to guarantee this right in the Constitution and without any need to change the Constitution, it was very easy for lawmakers to limit this right. This happened with the modification of the Compulsory Education Act in 1969. The right to home education was effectively eliminated, as it was limited to parents who disagreed with the confessional basis of the schools in their neighbourhood. This change converted home education from a fully accepted form of education based on the philosophical and pedagogical considerations of parents, into an escape route for 'religious school refusers'. The fact that home education is still a fully-fledged form of education in many other countries in the world, and is even growing rapidly in popularity, did not prove to be an argument[22].

Extending the years of compulsory education

In 1969 the age limit for compulsory schooling was raised to fifteen. In 1975 compulsory education was increased to the age of sixteen, and in 1985 it was lowered to require five year olds to attend school. In 2007, compulsory qualifications were introduced for sixteen and seventeen year olds. Compulsory qualification means that children

---

[22] Homeschooling Research: www.hslda.org

who are not 'qualified', who do not have a diploma, are forced to stay in school. Nor does the law stop there, since 2009 'unqualified' people are also excluded from social welfare until aged twenty-seven, and actively tracked by school attendance officers. In 2014 there were even discussions in parliament about increasing the age for compulsory education to twenty-one[23,24].

The expansion of funding requirements for schools

From 1848 to 1917 'the school struggle' raged in the Netherlands. The school struggle was about the government funding of private Protestant and Catholic schools. After seventy years of political struggle these religious groups had managed to get their schools funded by the government in 1917. Article 23 of the Constitution was expanded to give the legislature powers to determine the criteria for funding. The legislature has increasingly made use of these powers. The funding requirements for schools are specified in acts on primary and secondary schooling. In the early 1990s core objectives were added[25]. These are the goals that every school must have. These state-imposed objectives severely limit the freedom of schools to formulate their own objectives. In 2014 the requirements to assess learning

[23] http://www.nu.nl/politiek/3713212/pvda-wil-leerplicht-verlengen-21.html
[24] https://d2vry01uvf8h31.cloudfront.net/Personen/rog/MvT_Initiatiefwetsvoorstel_Verlening_Kwalificatieplicht_Jadnanansing_en_Rog.pdf
[25] Kamerstukken II, 1990-1991, 20381, nr 141

outcomes and minimum reference levels for students were added. The straitjacket in which schools are being squeezed is becoming ever tighter.

Phantom Legislation

In 2002 the Education Inspection Act was passed. This act governs how the school inspection executes its oversight, and formulates a number of assumptions to this end. These create a number of additional, non-legal requirements for schools. In addition to the legal requirements, schools now need to meet a number of 'quality rules'. Formally the schools do not have to meet these rules, after all they are not funding requirements, but in practise the school inspectorate uses these to inspect schools, and they do not differentiate between the two categories. Schools thus have little choice than to meet all the requirements. If not, they are nailed to a virtual pillory - a list of (very) weak schools that appears on the government website.

This problem of unclear requirements for schools is aggravated by the fact that the funding requirements are not clear standards, but so-called target regulations[26,27]. Target regulations only provide targets for schools, not clear norms. An example of target regulation in traffic regulation

---

[26] Timmer, W., (2011), Het Doel wel gesteld, dissertatie 30642 EUR: repub.eur.nl
[27] Kamerstukken II, 2014–2015, 33862, nr. 2, Initiatief wetsvoorstel; Beter toezicht, beter onderwijs

would be that cars must maintain a 'safe' speed. A clear norm would be a specifically defined speed limit for cars. The requirement to keep a safe speed would allow police to hand out fines to motorists if their speed was 'unsafe'. Giving a fine would then be based on the personal interpretation of the police officer, rather than an objective measurement. Target legislation in education makes determining whether a school meets a legal criterion a personal matter for the individual inspectors. In his PhD thesis, lawyer Wim Timmer concludes that target legislation always results in far-reaching interpretations of the legal requirements by inspectors. As a consequence schools not only need to meet the legal requirements, but also the (personal) interpretation of the law made by the school inspectors. The Dijsselbloem commission called this 'phantom legislation'[28], which formally does not apply to schools, but which must be followed in practice. Little freedom remains for schools. That this can result in great infringements into the educational liberty of children and parents is obvious.

The misfortunes of two private schools that tried to defend their constitutional rights against the government.

In theory, private, non-subsidised schools have more freedom. They receive no government funding and therefore

---

[28] Kamerstukken II, 2007–2008, 31007 nr 6,'Rapport parlementaire enquêtecommissie Dijsselbloem naar het falen van 20 jaar onderwijsvernieuwing'.

do not need to meet the funding requirements. For parents who want a different education for their children, establishing a school themselves is the only option left by the Compulsory Education Act. Case law from the Supreme Court consistently refers to this option when an appeal by home educating parents is rejected[29].

Between 2007 and 2014, the parents, students and founders of two private schools tried to protect their pedagogical vision from government interference. This proved to be impossible. In 2012 even the Council of State, the highest administrative court, did not see any objections to upholding decisions on the basis of inspection reports, which were based on phantom legislation. The burden of proof in administrative law is rather vague, and proving that the government has done something wrong is next to impossible. The parents were left empty handed, as the Council of State judged the actions of the government to have been 'reasonable'. Based on the principle of 'unity of law' the criminal courts followed this decision. As result the parents of two private schools, De Kampanje in Amersfoort, De Koers in Beverwijk, were criminally convicted in 2014 for enrolling their children in these schools. This forced these schools to close their doors. The constitutional freedom of education had slipped like sand between their

---

[29] Zie o.a. HR 11 februari 2003, LJN: AF0453, r.o. 7.6, betreffende het verbod op huisonderwijs en het recht om zelf een school te starten. Zie in dit verband voorts HR 4 juli 2006, LJN: AX8639, r.o. 20 en HR 15 februari 2011, LJN: BM6898, r.o. 5.5.

fingers. The Constitution did not offer any protection to parents against interference by the government.

In the remainder of this book, I will show the effects of this lack of protection of the constitutional freedom of education: state education and state coercion at the expense of children, at the expense of parents and at the expense of teachers.

MYTHS IN COERCIVE EDUCATION

Education is very important and therefore discussions are often quite intense. The way people see education is largely determined by their own values and assumptions, however these values and assumptions are rarely mentioned in discussions about education. Such discussions are mostly concerned with the way education is provided in practice, or the 'how' of teaching and schooling. After five generations of people who are 'products' of the education system, fundamental questions are no longer being asked: Why do we have education? Why do we have year groups? Why do we constantly test children? Why is education coercive? Why do children need guidance? Why do we have diplomas? Why is there so much bullying in schools? These questions are just as fundamental as asking why the earth rotates around the sun, why there is gravity, and why the leaves on trees are green? Without asking these fundamental questions it is not possible to improve the education system, or to develop education on the basis of entirely different pedagogical visions.

In this chapter I will review some myths of coercive education. I use the word 'myth' here in the sense of a belief, which, when looked at objectively, proves to be incorrect. Through these myths, a number of assumptions regarding the current education system are questioned. The insights that emerge create an opportunity to develop new visions of education.

Myth 1 - More education is better

The answer given to the call to improve education is often: more education. This is then translated to enhanced supervision, more subjects, longer school days and shorter holidays. There have even been long discussions in the Dutch parliament about a minimum number of school hours, lowering the age at which education becomes coercive and the introduction of coercive education for adults aged eighteen to twenty-seven years.

In recent decades, the amount of tax money invested annually in education has grown enormously. The government's Social and Cultural Planning Office has calculated that between 1998 and 2009, in real terms (i.e. after inflation) the cost of primary education has increased by 63% and that of secondary education by 46%, with very few qualitative improvements to be seen[30]. The quality of primary education has remained the same and the quality of secondary education has increased a little. It was decided in 2007 to spend an extra 1.1 billion euros to improve the quality of teachers[31]. A report, the Periodic Survey, by the Office for Research in Education in the Netherlands states that 40-50% of children in primary schools do not meet the required standards[32]. In a large-scale pilot study for a central arithmetic test in 2012, involving almost 80,000 pupils, almost 60% failed the test[33]. Approximately 10% of the Dutch population is illiterate or has low literacy[34,35] and a similar percentage can barely do sums. These are people have been coerced at school for more than 9 years. Many people agree that there is a serious problem, and the

[30] Sociaal en Cultureel Planbureau, 2012, 'Waar voor ons belastinggeld? Prijs en kwaliteit van publieke diensten'
[31] NRC 20-03-2008
[32] Schoot, F. Van der, PPON, 2008, 'Onderwijs op peil?, Een samenvattend onderzoek van 20 jaar', Cito Arnhem
[33] Pilot rekentoets in vo en examens taal en rekenen mbo, brief minister van Onderwijs aan Tweede Kamer 8 juni 2012
[34] Wikipedia, laaggeletterdheid: nl.wikipedia.org
[35] Stichting lezen en schrijven, (2014), Feiten & cijfers geletterdheid Overzicht van de gevolgen van laaggeletterdheid en opbrengsten van investeringen voor samenleving en individu.

question is whether this problem will be solved with more forced education.

In this context it is interesting to look at the effects of **less** coercive education, for which there are some notable examples. In the 1930s, the superintendent of a number of primary schools in Manchester, New Hampshire, USA, decided to undertake an experiment on the effects of less education[36]. He eliminated arithmetic lessons for a number of classes in a number of schools, for grades one to five. At the beginning of their sixth grade year, the children who had not been taught any arithmetic, performed much better on story problems that could be solved by common sense and a general understanding of numbers and measurement and scored lower on standard arithmetic tests. However by the end of grade 6, they scored equal on the standards test and still much higher on story problems.

A similar result was found in Denmark recently[37]. Due to a conflict between the teacher unions and the Minister of Education in 2013, teachers in Danish high schools were not allowed into the schools for a month, and the students did not receive any education at school. Teachers unions were outraged about this. They warned of the catastrophic effects

[36] Benezet, L. P. (1935/1936). The teaching of Arithmetic: The Story of an Experiment. Originally published in Journal of the National Education Association in three parts. Vol. 24, #8, pp 241-244; Vol. 24, #9, p 301-303; & Vol. 25, #1, pp 7-8.
[37] Jyllands Posten, 11-11-2013 eksamenskarakterer steg trods lockout: jyllands-posten.dk

of the closure of schools on students preparing for their final exams. The students sat the exams and the results proved even to be better than in previous years. One month less education led to higher exam results!

An education expert from New Zealand had predicted these positive effects. In February 2011 a severe earthquake hit the city of Christchurch. School buildings were severely damaged and could not be used. As a result the students preparing for their final exams could not go to school for four months. The New Zealand Qualifications Authority had already made preparations to offset the expected lower exam grades by 'an earthquake correction factor' for the exams. This turned out to be unnecessary. A local newspaper headline read: *'Students in Christchurch achieve the best results'*[38]. These seem to be no coincidence. The Dutch Central Bureau of Statistics shows, in a elaborate study of the PISA results (2015), that there is a positive correlation between shorter teaching time and better learning performance. A national newspaper headline read: *'Improved academic performance through less school'*[39].

> IMPROVED ACADEMIC RESULTS THROUGH LESS SCHOOL

---

[38] The Press, 16-1-2012, Christchurch pupils achieve best results: www.stuff.co.nz
[39] Baars, L. van, Trouw, 26-1-2015, 'Betere leerprestaties door minder lesuren': www.trouw.nl

The theory that more education is better is false. There is no scientific basis for our present coercive education, let alone that more education would be even better. There are indications that less coercive education is better. The question is, why coercive education is considered right anyway, and why all children between the ages of four and eighteen must spend the larger part of their youth under duress at school. The rights of children are being violated through increased education.

Myth 2 - Teaching is learning

If you have children who have just undertaken a chosen activity and ask them 'What have you learned?' they often say: 'Nothing'. Why is that?

After more than a hundred years of coercive education, this question is not interpreted as 'What have you learned?' but 'What have you been taught?' and if there is no teacher involved, or if there has not been a teaching situation, the answer is usually 'nothing'. The philosopher Ivan Illich explains in his book *Deschooling Society* that schools are very effective in teaching children that they can only learn if they are taught[40].

Where the original meaning of learning is about expanding your personal knowledge, insights and skills, these days 'learning' is mostly interpreted as being 'taught', or attending 'class'. It is of course possible for learning to occur during a lesson, but most learning happens outside the formal classroom. Or in the words of Mark Twain:

'I never let my schooling interfere with my education'.

Winston Churchill was also very clear about the difference between teaching and education:

'Schools have not necessarily much to do with education ... they are mainly institutions of control where certain basic habits must be inculcated to the young. Education is quite different and has little place in school.'

The concept of education as stipulated in the international human rights treaties has much broader scope than being simply the right to be taught or schooled.

---

[40] Illich, I., (1970), Deschooling society, Marion Boyars Publishers Ltd.

Education also stands for self-development, learning and acquiring knowledge and skills. Teaching is mainly limited to instruction. Learning is an individual activity that takes place in the head and/or body. Teaching can affect learning, but rarely with the intended results. A kilo of teaching almost never results in a kilo of learning.

> A KILO OF TEACHING NEVER RESULTS IN A KILO OF LEARNING

With the rise of authoritarian ideas around the end of the nineteenth century, coercive education became synonymous with the learning of people between the ages of five and eighteen years. People under five years and over eighteen years learn in a natural way or have the free choice to develop themselves and in the way they want[41].

As a result of evolution, humans are naturally curious and inquisitive. They were able to survive as a species by rapidly adapting to the environment and conditions. This required good use of their brain capacity and this capacity developed further through evolution. It is often said that children are lazy and will not to learn by themselves, and this often refers to children who already have been coerced in school for a period of time. If the coercion disappears these

---

[41] Thomas, A. & Pattison, H., (2007), How Children Learn at Home, Continuum Publishing Group

children will indeed do nothing for a limited amount of time, because they need time to switch from being externally directed to self-direction.

People under the age of four use their abilities to the fullest and do not take walking or talking lessons. They teach themselves to walk and talk. Children who are not exposed to forced education know what is important to them and will take appropriate action. Babies are always busy and are never called lazy. Most people above eighteen also learn in a natural way, and decide for themselves whether they want to do a course or undertake specific training. Learning is often the by-product of the activities they do.

Peter Gray demonstrates that children know what is important to them in his book *Free to Learn*[42]. This book uses an extreme example to show that children are not just playing. Peter Gray describes how a group of children in a Nazi concentration camp played a game to practice dealing with the guards. They played this game, not because they enjoyed it, but to survive. It is important that these children did so without any interference from adults.

You can learn from coercive education, but most learning happens without coercion. Scientific research shows that even in coercive education more than 80% of learning has

---

[42] Gray, P., (2013), Free to Learn, Basic Books

nothing to do with the education and is invisible[43]. Forced education deprives children of time to learn and therefore violates the right of the child to develop.

[43] Moravec, J. & Cobo, C., (2011), Invisible Learning, http://www.aprendizajeinvisible.com/

Myth 3 - Coercive education prevents child labour

Child labour, or rather, the exploitation and abuse of children by adults, is not allowed. It is a violation of the rights of children, to force them to work long hours in unhealthy factories. If children have to work all week, they cannot enjoy their right to education.

In the Netherlands one of the first steps against exploitation of children was the Child Act proposed by van Houten in 1874. This act prohibited children under the age of twelve from working in factories. The introduction of the Compulsory Education Act in 1902 is often presented as a further step in the realisation of children's rights. The Compulsory Education Act forced all parents who were unable to home educate them to send children aged between six and twelve years to school. Since 1902 the law has thus guaranteed that children could realise their right to education.

If we compare the enforced stay in a school with working in a factory, is school so much better? Labour inspector Helen M. Todd (1913) from Chicago, USA, studied children working in harsh and difficult conditions in factories, and of the 500 children surveyed, 412 preferred working in a sweatshop to attending school because of the monotony, humiliation and cruelty in schools[44].

How does enforced labour in school currently compare to working in a factory? The problem is that we cannot ask the children themselves any more, because they have been

---

[44] Fraknoi, A., (2007), Societal Impact of Spaceflights, NASA 2007, Chapter 21, Space Science Education in the US, the good, the bad and the ugly, p 408: history.nasa.gov

excluded from work since the introduction of coercive education, but we still can look at the conditions in which students are working at school and compare these with the conditions in which that people work in today's businesses.

Compared to 100 years ago, today's working conditions are quite comfortable. The number of hours worked has fallen sharply, there are many breaks, ergonomic conditions have greatly improved, working with hazardous substances has become much safer, cleanliness has increased significantly, there is clean air, free from dust etc. Additionally, employers, who fear losing their better workers to competitors, have a vested interest in the welfare of their employees. If workers are bullied at work, become burnt out or stressed, it is the obligation of the employer to act. If employers fail to act, employees can go to court and demand damages. Many employers and businesses realise that it is in their self-interest to ensure that their employees are happy and can develop themselves. Happy employees tend to be more productive and will not move to a competitor.

What is the working environment like in today's schools? Is a school a healthy environment? Are children protected by a maximum of working hours? Do children have sufficient breaks? Do all schools have ergonomically sound furniture? Are children protected from hazardous substances such as asbestos? Are the schools hygienic and is the air clean? Are children protected against bullying, stress and burnout? Do children have access to legal means to protect themselves

39

when their rights are infringed? Do children have a free choice to go to school or to decide what they do inside the school? Do they have the right not to do something? If we look at the newspapers and the debates in Parliament over the last twenty years, we can easily conclude that not everything works well in schools.

Children are often situated in poorly maintained and unsanitary buildings with poor air quality[45]. In school, they are forced every day to do things they have not chosen for themselves. They have long working days, not least because of all the homework they must complete. Children, who cannot maintain the pace, often have to finish their work during breaks or after school hours. Children in school are also at risk of physical and/or psychological abuse as a result of bullying[46]. Children who are struggling to get along or have different ideas about their education are dismissed as having 'problem behaviour' or 'psychological problems' (labelled with ADHD, ADD, etc.). These children are often given drugs to allow them to function within the school system. Where companies have a duty to care for the welfare of their employees, in schools it is often the children themselves who are blamed for the problems they face.

---

[45] 'In 80% van de klaslokalen schiet de lucht kwaliteit ernstig tekort': http://www.co2indicator.nl/scholen.html
[46] 10% van de kinderen wordt op school gepest, Pestcijfers: www.saqi.nl

A teacher wanted to experience how what it was like to be student and decided to participate for two days as a student in her own school. Her experiences can be read in a blog from the Washington Post[47]:

> *'I could not believe how tired I was after the first day'*

> *'I could not stop yawning and I was desperate to move or stretch'*

> *'I was drained, and not in a good, long, productive-day kind of way. No it was that icky, lethargic tired feeling, (...) I was so drained I couldn't do anything that involved mental effort (so instead I watched TV) and I was in bed by 8:30.*

> *'It was not just the sitting that was draining but that so much of the day was spent absorbing information but often not grappling with it'*

> *'It made me realize how little autonomy students have, how little of the learning they are directing or choosing'*

> *'Teachers work hard, but I now think that conscientious students work harder'*

At school, children are forced all day to do things they do not choose for themselves, and they are forced to think in a certain way. The laws and regulations that protect workers in companies are virtually absent for children in school. Because the government forces children to go to school and

---

[47] Strauss, V., 24-10-2014, Teacher spends two days as a student and is shocked at what she learned, Washington post: www.washingtonpost.com

decides via the curriculum what children must learn, schools have little incentive to improve the working conditions of children, to prevent bullying effectively, to clean the buildings, to ensure good air quality or to provide each individual child with an education that really interests them. Similarly, the Trabant factory in the former Eastern bloc had no incentive to improve the quality of their car. School is thus comparable to child labour. According to the rights of the child, child labour is prohibited. Forced education is a violation of this right.

> SCHOOL IS SIMPLY CHILD LABOUR.

Myth 4 - Education is diverse

The educational system of the Netherlands is diverse, according to previous Minister of Education Maria van der Hoeven (2004), and she is not the only one to say so. The constitutional freedom of education allows anyone to start a school, and that has happened often. Two-thirds of all schools in the Netherlands are more or less private; formally owned by private institutions, but funded and regulated by the state. Internationally the diversity of the Dutch education system is praised and there is indeed much more diversity than in other countries, not only in comparison with countries such as North Korea or the former Soviet Union, but also compared to countries such as Spain or France. Glenn and De Groof (2012) note[48]: *'The Dutch can justly claim they have the most pluralistic school system in the world.'*

But how diverse is the education system in the Netherlands? If education is more diverse than in countries such as Spain and France, this may simply indicate that there is even less diversity in those countries. That seems a much more reasonable assumption, because in these countries education is run almost entirely by the state. This can be

---

[48] Zoontjes, P.J.J. & Glenn, C.L. (2012) The Netherlands. In: Balancing Freedom, Autonomy and Accountability in Education, Eds. Glenn, C. & Groof, J., Wolf Publishers, Nijmegen. 333-362

compared with the East German citizen who could choose from one type of Trabant and was still better off than the North Korean who was never able to afford a car. More grey colours do not create a rainbow.

When Article 23 of the Constitution, was amended in 1917 to allow the public funding of private schools, the words 'education' and 'upbringing' were used interchangeably. Freedom was real freedom and meant that there was no interference by the state. Politicians realised that freedom in education was essential to the welfare and prosperity of the country, because freedom guarantees a diverse educational system and unrestrained innovation. An example of the effects of freedom can be seen in the Netherlands in the seventeenth century. Freedom led to a period of unprecedented growth and prosperity compared to neighbouring countries, and this period is still called the Golden Age for that reason.

To maintain diversity in education, it is essential that parents have the freedom to decide how they raise their children. It is always necessary to prevent the state from controlling the upbringing and education of children, because otherwise we are not far from the North Korean model of state education and state indoctrination. In the words of Paul Zoontjes, Professor of Education Law: 'Nobody in the Netherlands knows what good education is. Therefore, there is freedom of education'[49].

This freedom of education only exists in theory. Article 120 of the Constitution prevents courts from testing laws against the Constitution[50]. This gives parliament the ability to limit the constitutional freedom of education and in its wisdom, parliament has made extensive and enthusiastically use of this ability over the past 100 years. The Inspector General for Education, Prof. Dr. F. Mertens, noted in a farewell

---

[49] Kamerstukken II, 2014/2015, 33 862, nr. 5
[50] Hirsch Ballin in video over artikel 23 GW, van de Raad van de Rechtspraak: www.youtube.com

interview in 2002 that all schools were forced into a straitjacket[51].

As the result of further and more detailed education acts in parliament, all schools today offer the standard curriculum, use similar teaching methods, test students and have student surveillance systems where they keep the details of every single student. Previously innovative educational movements such as Montessori, Dalton and Jena were also forced to conform and are increasingly difficult to distinguish from other schools. Today they are called the 'traditional innovators'. The question is: what is the meaning of the word 'innovator'? The diversity of education increasingly resembles the diversity of modern shopping centres. The diversity of local shops disappears at the expense of the large chain stores that sell the same range of products in each city. If you are in a shopping centre between these chain stores you do not know which city you are in any more.

> SCHOOLS ARE FORCED INTO A STRAITJACKET

Overregulation of education by the government has led to serious problems, so serious that in 2007 the Dutch

---

[51] Mertens, F, 2001, Interview in de Volkskrant 13-1-2013: 'Verstarring op school, De scholen klagen dat de politiek hen in een dwangbuis heeft gestopt. Scheidend inspecteur-generaal Ferdinand Mertens, de hoogste baas van de onderwijsinspectie, geeft hun gelijk': www.volkskrant.nl

Parliament decided to have a full parliamentary inquiry into the government-led educational reforms of the last 20 years, the Dijsselbloem commission.

The National Ombudsman wrote an article on the conclusions of this parliamentary inquiry in the Government Gazette: *'The report of the Dijsselbloem commission shows that the concern of the government with education has gone way too far. According to Chairman Dijsselbloem, the party political interests were put over and above the interests of the children'*[52].

Little was done with the recommendations of the Dijsselbloem commission, according to the Council for Education, a government appointed education advisory body[53]. Parliament and the Ministry of Education continue to meddle in detail with the content and manner of teaching and they continue to

> **PARTY POLITICAL INTERESTS ARE PUT OVER AND ABOVE THE INTERESTS OF CHILDREN**

develop even more laws to regulate education. That all these new laws do little to solve the problems can be seen from

---

[52] Brenninkmeijer, A.,F.,M., (2008), Vrijheid van onderwijs onderbelicht, Staatscourant 18 februari 2008
[53] Onderwijsraad, (2014), Onderwijspolitiek na de commissie-Dijsselbloem: www.onderwijsraad.nl

the fact that no structural improvements have occurred in education.

A few party spokespersons for education in parliament actually did see the damaging effects of these extensive and on-going government interventions. They initiated a proposed law called *Better education through better inspection*[54], which will force the government to inspect schools only according to the legal requirements and not by any other criterion. In 2014, the Council of State, the government advisory body on legislation, issued a positive recommendation, but they still questioned whether this law was radical enough. It is a very important law to protect the freedom of education.

After his term as Inspector General for Education, Mertens was tasked, as the Inspector General for transportation, to modernise inspection. One of the things he did was to design new oversight of air traffic, which is now set-up very professional and in line with oversight internationally. When visiting an innovative school he was surprised about how the school inspectorate worked and he stated: *'Every inspection system tends to standardize and the challenge is how to handle the exceptions'*[55].

[54] Kamerstukken II, 2014-2015, 33 862, nr. 5
[55] Petitie van 4 democratische scholen aan parlement 23-11-2011

The conclusion is that diversity in education is very limited in the Netherlands and that standardised inspections result in even less diversity. This lack of diversity deprives children of choices in their education. Children are never consulted when new laws are made about their education, although the Convention of the Rights of the Child requires that children be heard in all important decisions that affect them.

Myth 5 - Testing results in better education

Testing is a tool that is widely used in coercive education. There is nothing wrong with the tests themselves. If you want to test your knowledge or want to know how proficient you are, you can use a test. The number of correct and incorrect answers can give an indication of what you have mastered and what you have not. A student uses tests as a tool in this way.

In coercive education tests have become the objective, and are no longer a tool for students.

> **TESTS HAVE BECOME THE OBJECTIVE**

Tests are mainly used to measure the effectiveness of teaching itself. To do so, schools have made tests compulsory for students and have little choice because the government has forced them to do so. Inspections check the test results of a school and if they are above the norm, the school will not be bothered. If the results are below the norm additional inspections will follow. This measure has, probably unintentionally, disastrous effects on the learning opportunities and development of children. All schools now test extensively, and the teachers are also judged on 'their' test results, that is, the test scores of the children who are forced to take the tests. The fact that schools and teachers are made accountable for the test results of individual pupils puts a lot of pressure on the students, with stress as a result.

The effect of this system is that teachers can do little other than prepare 'their' students for the tests as well as possible.

Their work turns increasingly into teaching to the test[56]. The main value of testing, however, is that it provides an indication of how well a student will do on the next test[57]. The question is of course what this has to do with the learning and development of students.

Most tests check whether children can reproduce what they have been told in class by the teacher. This is not just about reproducing facts, but also views and ways of thinking. Claire Boonstra, the initiator of Operation Education, showed in her TEDx talk the effect of systems in which children are trained to provide the desired responses[58]. She gives the example of her nephew Casper, answering a question from the Cito[59] test, a national test, for five-year olds. Casper is presented with a picture of an igloo and he has to choose between red for hot and blue for cold. He chooses red. His argument is that inside the igloo it is warmer than outside, however, Cito has determined that the right answer is blue on the grounds that an igloo is always in a cold place. On this basis, Cito concludes that Casper obviously does not knows what an igloo is. If Casper wants to be successful in school he has to adapt his thinking to the Cito logic. As a result, children are forced to adjust their

[56] Trouw, 9-5-2015, 'Het Eindexamen heeft zijn beste tijd gehad': www.trouw.nl

[57] Master, S., (2015), 7 things every kid should master, Boston Globe, 26-02-2015

[58] Claire Boonstra on the Shift to Value-Centered Education at TEDxAmsterdamED 2012: www.youtube.com

[59] Cito, the gouvernement Central Institute for Test Development

thinking to what the designers of the tests have determined as 'good' answers. So tests not only force children to provide the desired answers, but go much further. This is the conditioning of the thinking of children; a thought police through testing. That the answers of the test designers are not always the only right answers, speaks for itself. For most questions there are of course several possible answers, all of which may be correct, but are usually not considered correct.

A good example of how this 'thought police' functions, can be found in the book *Turning Learning Right Side Up* by Russell L. Ackoff and Daniel Greenberg[60]. During a physics exam, a student receives the following question from their teacher: Suppose you are in a tall building and you have an accurate barometer. How would you use it to determine the height of the building?

> *'Everyone with some basic knowledge of physics will understand that the student is expected to give the answer to measure the air pressure at the top of the building and measure the air pressure at the bottom of the building and then calculate the height via the formula, which gives the relation between the two.*
> *The student is an independent thinker, who finds it demeaning to provide such an obvious answer. So he*

---

[60] Ackoff, R.L. & Greenberg, D., (2008), 'Turning learning right side up; putting education back on track', Wharfton School Publishing

answers: 'Tie a string to the barometer, lower it down the side of the building, and measure the string'. The teacher is not happy with this answer and gives the student another chance. He provides a number of answers: 'You can measure the shadow and the length of the barometer, and then measure the shadow of the building, and use the ratio of shadow-to-length to figure out the height of the building. You can just drop the barometer over the side of the building and figure out the height by the time it takes to hit the ground. You can make a pendulum from the barometer and measure the gravitational force exerted by measuring the swing, calculate the force of Earth's gravity, which lessens as you get away from the Earth, thus determining the height of the building. You can climb down the fire escape, using the barometer as a ruler, and mark off the building's height in barometer lengths'. All these answers are judged to be wrong. The student strongly protests and gets one last chance.

He still does not want to conform to the teacher and answers: 'you can go to the janitor and tell him that you'll give him this beautiful new barometer if he tells you the height of the building'.

This story is a perfect example of the intellectual straitjacket in which forced education tries to enclose the minds of children. One of the consequences is that the creativity all children are born with is seriously damaged. The education critic Sir Ken Robinson is very clear here in his TED talk *Do schools kill creativity?*[61]

Forced testing seems to have run out of control in the Netherlands[62,63], but it can get much worse. One country that has a lot of experience forced testing is the US. In her book *Contradictions of School*

> COERCIVE EDUCATION IS AN INTELLECTUAL STRAITJACKET FOR CHILDREN

Reform, Educational Costs of Standardized Testing, Professor Linda M. McNeil of Rice University shows that the pressure on schools to show good test results decreases both the quality and quantity of children's learning[64]. Based on extensive research she comes to the conclusion that the more children are tested, the less they learn.

On an international level, educational outcomes are compared in three annual surveys of the OECD (Organisation for Economic Co-operation and Development), the PISA surveys[65]. Finland is praised by many for its good education system and the country tops the

---

[61] Robinson, K., (2006), Do schools kill creativity? : www.youtube.com

[62]Stop de doorgeslagen toetscultuur (2015): groenlinks.nl

[63] Brandpunt 24 november 2013, Reportage: De macht van de toets. Wordt er te veel getoetst?

[64] McNeil, L.M. , (2000), Contradictions of school reform, Educational costs of Standardized testing, Routledge

[65] The Programme for International Student Assessment (PISA) www.oecd.org

Pisa rankings. In Finland it is understood how much damage forced testing causes[66]. Here it is forbidden by law to test children less than eight years of age and children under sixteen years of age can only be tested if they choose it themselves.

Testing children who do not choose to do such tests themselves does not lead to better education. On the contrary, forced testing has a detrimental effect on the learning and development of children. Forced tests infringe the right of the child to develop.

[66] 'National Opt Out Day' Rejects Standardized Tests – Huffington Post February 20, 2013: www.huffingtonpost.com

Myth 6 - Children need guidance

Many adults judge children as incompetent and therefore think that children should be guided and controlled. This assumption is so strong that over the last hundred years it has been firmly anchored in the education laws and regulations. This guidance and control is aimed at preparing children for a life in which they are supposed to be self-reliant, can contribute to society and can take responsibility.

Self-reliance and personal responsibility, explained in this way or another, is hardly ever a subject for debate. Self-reliance and responsibility are even reflected in the human rights treaties, however, the question of how these goals can be best achieved is subject to fierce debate.

Children are not only forced by law to spend more and more hours in school, but within school the guidance of children (a friendly way to express coercion) is increasing. More and more subjects are added to the curriculum and the number of mandatory tests keeps increasing. Where in the Netherlands in the late 1960s one central test was introduced at the end of primary school, children now take two central tests per subject per year. That's about seventy central tests throughout their primary school careers, and then there are the tests that are part of the teaching 'methods', which are multiples of this. For example, at a typical primary school in Rotterdam, children have to take two hundred and forty of these tests over their school career[67].

The assumption underlying this increase in coercion is that children are simply not competent enough to decide for themselves what is important to them, and therefore adults have to intervene, but is this assumption true?

Competencies define what people can achieve. Competencies are evolutionarily determined, but more than a hundred years of coercive education have deprived children many opportunities to develop. After all, nowadays, children can do little else, as they are forced to go to school. Children now have hardly any opportunities to show

> OVER 100 YEARS OF COERCIVE EDUCATION HAVE DEPRIVED CHILDREN OF MANY POSSIBILITIES TO DEVELOP

great achievements. The question is: what is the cause and what is the effect? In other words, are children incompetent and must they therefore be controlled, or are children deprived of opportunities to achieve and are therefore seen

---

[67] Source: teacher at a primary school in Rotterdam, the Netherlands.

as incompetent (and must therefore be controlled even more)?

In his book *Case Against Adolescence*, the psychologist Robert Epstein shows, based on extensive research, that children from the age of twelve to fourteen are as competent as adults[68].

He studied competencies such as intelligence, memory, speed of reaction and moral judgment in detail. He convincingly shows that people are at their most competent around their fourteenth year, and that their skills from thereon steadily decline. The competences of an eighty year old are, on average, at the level of an eight or ten year old.

He shows many examples of people who have made achievements at a very young age that most people would consider impossible. Bobby Fischer became a chess grandmaster at the age of twelve and he was not even the youngest person to do so, and there are many more examples. Many of these examples stem from a time when children were not forced to sit in school until they were eighteen. Michiel de Ruyter, the Dutch Admiral who beat the English fleet several times, was eleven years old when he joined the navy and he was fifteen years old when he had reached the rank of skipper. Skipper is the highest non-

---

[68] Epstein, R., Ph.D., (2007), Case Adolescence, Rediscovering the Adult in Every Teen, Quill Driver Books/Word Dancer Press, Inc.

commissioned officer rank in the navy. The prominent seventeenth century mathematician and scientist Christiaan Huygens was sixteen years old when he went to study at Leiden University. Hugo Grotius, the 17th century lawyer who wrote 'Mare Librium' the basis of today's international law, went to study in Leiden aged eleven, and established himself as a lawyer in the Hague when he was seventeen.

Recently, Laura Dekker sailed solo around the world, starting at the age of fourteen and finishing when she was sixteen, something few adults will do. A few years ago, a national newspaper, the NRC published a series of articles about young entrepreneurs like Ben Woldring, who started a comparison website for mobile phones when he was thirteen. Soon his company became so successful that he had to hire staff, including his mother. How much guidance and support did these young people need? Laura Dekker found her fight with the youth care services, who wanted her to attend school, much harder than sailing around the world on her own. Another young entrepreneur, Deniz Alkac was sixteen when he was offered a contract with broadcasting company BNN, and says in NRC in 2014 that he immediately left school when his mother called and told him that the attendance officer of the municipality gave permission[69].

The legislature has great confidence in the judgment and decision-making of children concerning ethics. Children in the Netherlands can, from twelve years old, decide on euthanasia, which requires a great awareness about this ethical issue. The same legislature does not allow children to decide how they want to prepare for their future, which requires a similar ethical awareness, but has much less impact on their lives.

Could it be that all guidance and control constitutes a barrier to young people taking responsibility?

---

[69] Zandstra, F., (2014), 16 jaar en een bloeiende onderneming, NRC.nl>weblogs>carriere: prev-m.nrc.nl

Daniel Greenberg, a founding member of the Sudbury Valley School, shows in his article *Do Children Need Guidance?* that forced guidance is destructive to the development of children and that only guidance at the request of children can be meaningful[70]. All babies and toddlers learn to walk and to talk by themselves, not because they learn this at school, but because they need this to survive in an environment where all their role models, such as parents, brothers and sisters, can talk and walk. What children learn by themselves is determined by the context they are in. If we were to prohibit children from learning to walk or talk at home and send them to a 'walking' or a 'talking school', we would not have to wait long before we were faced with gait disturbances and speech defects. Robert Epstein shows that this self-directed learning is not limited to walking and talking. He shows convincingly that when young people are given responsibility and control, they develop much faster than children who are continuously guided and controlled.

Children do not need to be guided as long as their environment offers opportunities for self-determined development. Guiding children means that they are forced to do things they do not want to do. Guidance is coercion and in most cases an obstacle to the growth and development of children. Children can, of course, ask for advice or for help, but then there is no control. Guidance hinders the

[70] Greenberg, D., (2014), Do Children need Guidance?, Sudbury Valley School Press. www.sudval.org

development of children and thereby violates the rights of the child.

Myth 7 - Education for democratic citizenship is provided at school

In recent decades, education for democratic citizenship has been high on the political agenda in Europe. The idea behind this is that we are living in a multicultural society and that we need to be able to live with people from many different backgrounds and cultures in a liberal society. Mutual respect, an understanding of democracy and the rule of law, and the ability to function therein are important.

Following the saying 'the twig is bent, so is the tree inclined', policy makers decided that education for democratic citizenship was crucial. In the 1990s the Council of Europe started initiatives for education for democratic citizenship, which were implemented in many countries in Europe. In the Netherlands in 2005 the education laws were amended to include education for democratic citizenship[71]. This has a few caveats.

Where the Council of Europe speaks about education for democratic citizenship, this is translated in the Netherlands as 'forming citizens'. Where talk at the European level is about educating people to function in a democracy, schools in the Netherlands are tasked with moulding citizens. These

---

[71] Staatsblad, Jaargang 2005, nr 678

are two very different things. To be able to function is rather different to being moulded. The latter appears to be more about pressing people into a mould designed by the government in the shape of a citizen.

Another question that can be asked is about an effective way to achieve the goal of education for democratic citizenship. Is it about knowing theory or about the ability to act in practice? Is it more important that children can pass a test on the Constitution, norms or values? Or do children need to be able to function in a multicultural democratic society? The first does not necessarily lead to the second, and sometimes even the opposite.

Barbera Oomen, Professor of Law and Pluralism, and member of the State Committee on the Constitution, calls for more education for democratic citizenship in the school practice[72]. The English school inspector, Derry Hannam, who has conducted research into effective ways of education for democratic citizenship for the British Ministry of Education, explained it more strongly and described the current education for democratic citizenship in schools as 'holiday planning in prison'[73,74], or learning in isolation and not being allowed to put it into practice. He also called for greater influence of pupils on school practice.

Schools are authoritarian environments in which children have virtually no say in issues such as the curriculum, tests,

[72] Oomen, B, (2009), Mensen en Kinderrechten: de gemiste kans van het burgerschapsonderwijs? NTOR nr 2.
[73] Hannam, D. (2001) A Pilot Study To Evaluate The Impact Of The Student Participation Aspects Of The Citizenship Order On Standards Of Education In Secondary Schools, A Report To The DFEE, London, CSV.
[74] Hannam, D. (2015), Lecture at Eudec conference, Poland.

rules and rule enforcement. They also have no access to a legal system to resolve abuse[75]. One may wonder how it is possible to have respect for children in an authoritarian environment. If 'respect' is defined as 'to take into account the feelings, needs and rights of others' there is no respect for children in coercive education.

> IN COERCIVE EDUCATION THERE IS LITTLE OR NO RESPECT FOR CHILDREN

Coercion and respect are diametrically opposed. There is an authority in schools that determines almost continuously what children must do. If current schools are regarded as mini-societies, they look more like communist dictatorships than the open and free Western societies that we know for people over eighteen. How are children supposed to learn to participate in

a democracy if they grow up in a dictatorial environment from their fourth until their eighteenth year? After the fall of the Berlin Wall in 1989, we saw how difficult this transition was for many adults, and sometimes still is. Why do we expect that children, when they are eighteen years old, can make this sudden change successfully?

Democratic schools show that schools do not need to be dictatorships[76]. Here children have real control over their

---

[75] A legal system within or outside the school. It is important that a child has access to a mechanism which solves abuse, without negative repercussions.

school, over the rules, rule enforcement and sometimes even the appointment of teachers. Some of these schools have existed with great success for more then ninety years. The world has not collapsed with the abolition of slavery, feudalism, absolute monarchy or the establishment of women's suffrage[77], so why is it so difficult to apply the principles of self-determination and individual freedom in schools? Forced education for democratic citizenship is the opposite of respect and learning to live with the values of human rights, and even violates those values. This coercion is itself always a violation of the rights of the child.

---

[76] European Democratic Education Community, www.eudec.org
[77] One of the arguments against suffrage was that woman are like children: constitutioncenter.org

Myth 8 - Diplomas guarantee success in life

Governments repeatedly hammer home the importance of qualifications. Leaving school without a diploma would be bad for children, and therefore, since 2007 in the Netherlands children between sixteen and eighteen have been forced to stay at school if they do not obtain a diploma (coercion to qualify), and people between eighteen and twenty-three are excluded from social benefits if they do not have a diploma. Schools also feel the diploma pressure. If schools show low exam results, they can be assessed by the school inspection as (very) weak. This means more intense surveillance by the inspection and possibly cuts in government subsidies. As a result of this pressure obtaining diplomas has become the goal of schools. Due to the strong pressure on schools to guarantee that all children obtain diplomas, teaching has become 'to the test'[78]. Schools have also started to exhibit strategic behaviour, for example, by reducing the school exam requirements or excluding children from exams or diverting children to a 'lower type' school[79].

---

[78] Vries, M. de, (2015), 'Het eindexamen heeft zijn beste tijd gehad', Trouw 9-5-2015

[79] Tweede Kamer, nr 33400 VIII - Vaststelling van de begrotingsstaten van het Ministerie van Onderwijs, Cultuur en Wetenschap (VIII) voor het jaar 2013

This is the cheapest and easiest way for schools to meet the requirements of the government.

While diplomas were originally just a means to gain access to further education, schools now increasingly focus on the diploma as a goal. That is what the government wants, but is this also good for learning and development of the school-age children themselves? What is the value of such a degree?

On the labour market, children cannot do much with their school diplomas. Companies attach little value to the different diplomas of secondary education. Possession of a diploma is never the main reason to hire someone. Diplomas may say something about how well children have reproduced what they have been taught, but diplomas say very little about skills, knowledge, experience, motivation and social skills.

The primary function of a diploma is to gain access to further education. The idea is that a diploma shows that someone is able to successfully finish further education, but this argument does not hold. Some years ago the teacher training colleges complained that many of their students were so bad at the Dutch language that they were actually unsuitable for training as a teacher and the Law Faculty of the Erasmus University in Rotterdam came to the conclusion that the law students were so poor at Dutch that they could not understand legal texts[80]. More recently, the same problem was detected with maths[81]. Obtaining a diploma is obviously no longer a guarantee of having obtained language or maths, which is adequate for further education. In general, a diploma, even with good marks, provides little guarantee of success in further education. The motivation of students appears to be a much better predictor of success. In his book *Flow* Mihaly Csikszentmihaly shows that

---

[80] Rechtenstudenten schrijven slecht Nederlands. De Volkskrant, 12 januari 2007: www.volkskrant.nl
[81] Taal en rekenen op school: www.rijksoverheid.nl

motivation is especially decisive for success[82]. Deci and Ryan also conclude that intrinsic motivation is one of the most critical factors for success[83].

Another aspect of the diploma requirement for further education is that diplomas may create a barrier. To obtain a diploma students must complete successfully a minimum number of courses[84]. If a child is not interested in some of the subjects, or if they have no aptitude for them (and these usually go together), this could result in failure to get a diploma and subsequent failure to be admitted to the further training of choice. If a particular subject is important for further education this is of course justified, but if the subject in question is irrelevant for following this further education, the diploma requirement can be a big barrier. Would not it be much better if further education institutes are able determine for themselves the requirements for the knowledge and skills of their prospective students?

Diplomas are not important for the successful future of young people. The content of qualifications is mainly based on what was seen as necessary in the past. Qualifications are no guarantee for the future, especially in a world that is changing faster and faster. As we saw above, schools focus

---

[82] Csikszentmihaly, M., (1991), 'Flow: The Psychology of Happiness', HarperCollins.
[83] Deci , R.L., Koestner, R.,& Ryan, R.M. (2001). Extrinsic rewards and intrinsic motivation in education: reconsidered once again. Review of Educational Research, 71 (1), 1-27.
[84] Voorbereidend wetenschappelijk onderwijs: nl.wikipedia.org

their teaching on the existing exam requirements. They can hardly do otherwise. This means that children are prepared for the past, rather than the future. Author, architect and expert in the field of learning and innovative organizations, Jef Staes, advocates diploma-free education. He writes that 'diploma thinking' is the basis of the failure of the current education system. He notes: *'Education and organizations have managed to change whole generations of students and staff into passionless, pension seeking sheep'*[85].

Technology and society changes very quickly and the rate of change is increasing. This requires different competencies. Diplomas come from a time in which knowledge and information was scarce. Diplomas were designed to test how much information a student can reproduce, however, information is

> ## DIPLOMAS COME FROM A TIME WHEN KNOWLEDGE AND INFORMATION WAS SCARCE

abundantly available now. For success in the future it is crucial to be able to find the right information quickly, to integrate this information with one's own knowledge, and to be able to successfully apply this newly developed knowledge.

---

[85] Staes, J., (2011), Ik was een schaap, Lanoo Campus/Scriptum.

So far diplomas appear to be an unreliable criterion for success in further education. A substantial number of students do not manage to complete these courses successfully. The number of students who drop out during further education continues to increase, despite all efforts, but there are many alternatives in order for institutes of higher education to select students who can successfully finish further education. Some programmes do this in part already, such as the Erasmus Medical Centre in Rotterdam, which selects students on the basis of talent and ambition[86].

Many art colleges take students based on their level of thinking, portfolio and motivation, via a 18+ test. Universities also accept students if they passed an entrance examination. This seems to work well, although for the student this has a huge disadvantage as the education laws force them to wait until they are twenty-one years of age to do so. There is no objective reason not to allow people of eighteen, sixteen or even fourteen years of age into university if they have passed this test.

Diplomas do not necessarily result in success in life, not even economic success. Diploma requirements exclude large groups of students with the right skills and motivation from further education. Diplomas have become the target rather than the means.

---

[86] Decentrale-selectie bij geneeskunde: www.erasmusmc.nl

Motivation is a much better predictor of success. For students in the Netherlands who do not want to obtain a diploma, the qualification requirement also results in a two-year day-jail sentence and the potential of missing out on two years of income[87].

> DIPLOMAS HAVE BECOME THE TARGET RATHER THAN THE MEANS

Mandatory diplomas exclude many young people from further education and thus hamper their development. This violates the rights of the child.

---

[87] Two years of day-prison is a severe punishment for the personal choice of not wanting a diploma, especially when compared with a recent case in which a drunk driver was sentenced to eighty hours of community service for killing three people.

Myth 9 - Teachers are treated as professionals

Teachers are the backbone of education. According to the Dutch government, nothing is more essential to the quality of education than the quality of teachers, and that there is room to improve this quality. In 2007 there was a parliamentary majority for an additional 1.1 billion euros annually to improve the quality of education and that the amount should fully benefit teachers. This is a substantial amount, even compared to the 16 billion euros allocated annually to primary and secondary education.

The parliamentary inquiry, the Dijsselbloem commission, which in 2008 examined the (failed) educational reforms of the last 20 years, concluded that the professionalism of schools and teachers must improve. Since then, all ministers for education have actively tried to achieve this, and the education sector itself is strongly in support. In 2011, a sector-wide agreement was reached between the Ministry of Education and the Council for Secondary Education, with the professionalism of teachers as the cornerstone. In 2015 a law was proposed to make the professional registration of teachers mandatory, because until then only 5% of teachers had registered[88].

---

[88] Wet op het leraren register (2015): www.internetconsultatie.nl

In his book *The Downfall of the Dutch Teacher* education expert and teacher, Ton van Haperen provides an indication of what teachers themselves think about their professionalism[89]. The title of his book already shows what he thinks. In 2015, the group 2032 Teacher was founded. The newspaper 'Trouw' reported: *'According to the 2032 Teacher group, teachers have far too little say about the curriculum. Due to the large amount of 'core objectives' with which schools have to comply, no flexibility is left to teachers and students complain about a lack of coherence in what they learn. This happens to the detriment of the quality of education and the job satisfaction of teachers'*[90].

The effect of government interference is also visible in other ways. Teachers are becoming less and less motivated. Education is the sector with the highest absenteeism[91]. Stress and burnout are common. Many teachers seem to continue to work in education despite, rather than thanks to, the government.

> TEACHERS ARE BECOMING LESS AND LESS MOTIVATED

Teacher training has also received attention from the government. The government wants to eliminate unqualified teachers in classrooms and to encourage more

---

[89] Haperen, T. van, (2007), De ondergang van de Nederlandse leraar, Nieuw Amsterdam.
[90] Vries, M. de, (2015), Leraren willen meer-te-zeggen krijgen over lesprogramma, Trouw 25-8-2015: www.trouw.nl
[91] CBS 24-11-2014.

teachers in secondary education to obtain university grades. To achieve this, many universities started with academic teacher training programmes. Aafke Romeijn, an unqualified teacher with a MSc in the Dutch language describes her experience of how these *'academic thinking, investigative professionals'* are trained in the magazine 'Vrij Nederland' *'Intelligence at zero and don't be too critical'*[92].

She reports: *'I've always been taught that an academic attitude is equivalent to independent thinking, but this principle is quickly and skilfully eradicated in the teacher training programme. Long before Christmas it became clear to me that I only had to do one thing: keep my eyes closed, lock down my brain and slavishly 'fill' the rubrics of the examination manual. (...) In effect, all you learn is how you can score sixes and sevens with as little effort as possible and how to best appease teachers. Is this what Sander Dekker, the Secretary of Education, means by educating academic teachers?'*

She talks about *'a measurement system that is sealed shut with protocols, measurements and rubrics by a government that is increasingly suspicious of teachers and the education sector'.* Her suggestion: *'Give (academic teacher training) space, freedom and autonomy, and ensure that future teachers can and dare to think autonomously, freely and*

---

[92] Romeijn, A., (2014), Verstand op nul en vooral niet te kritisch zijn, Vrij Nederland Rapportage, 19 december 2014: www.vn.nl

independently'. It seems that professional space is still hard to find even in the teacher training programmes.

As a former inspector general for education, Ferdinand Mertens noted in 2001 at his farewell, that schools are increasingly forced into a straitjacket[93]. Since then, this has only worsened. As schools are increasingly becoming stuck and are forced to do things they do not want to do, this also means that teachers have less and less freedom to act as professionals.

With all the new rules and regulations, the government seems to act based on distrust. Many new regulations result in additional controls. Teachers are caught between what their

> GOVERNMENT SEEMS TO ACT BASED ON DISTRUST

students need and what the government wants. Additional test and examination requirements have a direct impact on the freedom of teachers. These requirements force them to do more test and exam training, to the detriment of the teaching and learning time of students. The Dijsselbloem commission concluded that the government interferes in the pedagogy and didactics of the teachers, and even does so

---

[93] 'Verstarring op school', Volkskrant 13 januari 2001, Afscheidsinterview F. Mertens inspecteur generaal van het onderwijs.

without any legal basis[94]. In practice this mean that the government prescribes to teachers how to organise their teaching and how to teach.

This has not always been the case. Let us take a step back in time to ancient Greece. Socrates is considered the founder of Western philosophy. What would this philosophy look like if, 2500 years ago, the government of Athens had enforced the same rules and requirements for teachers as now in the Netherlands?

What would have happened if Socrates first had to get his teaching certificate at the University of Utrecht to be

[94] Onderwijsraad, (2014), Onderwijspolitiek na de commissie Dijsselbloem, www.onderwijsraad.nl

allowed to teach? What if the students of Socrates would not come to him of their own free will, but had to be arrested in the streets of Athens by the police and delivered to his school and coerced to follow his teachings? What if Socrates had been forced to spend a large portion of his time writing 'too late notes' and had to the design continuous learning plans, examine his students continuously, and constantly filling out the student monitoring system? And then write personal development plans for the students who scored below average?

If Socrates had been forced into such a straight jacket, how likely would he have been to found Western philosophy? That Western philosophy would even exist?

Socrates had professional space and he was valued for his competence. The Dutch teacher is trapped, despite all the talk about professionalism by the government, and sees theirs professional space diminishing all the time. If teachers are limited in their professionalism this is detrimental to the development of children, a fundamental children's right.

Myth 10 - You cannot experiment with children

Since the start of mass education people have been experimenting with different forms of education. This makes sense because from the time children have been forced to follow mass education, changing that education has been the only option. What binds many of the innovators is their aversion to coercing children.

Industrial mass education was invented and first used extensively in Prussia. From the beginning of 1800 Prussia was a military dictatorial state, which was admired by many for its efficiency and military power, not least in the relatively free countries in Northwest Europe and the US. All these countries have copied the Prussian education system in one way or another.

Leo Tolstoy was one of the first who, in the nineteenth century founded a school on the basis of absence of power and coercion, where the students were treated as thinking and rational human beings. In the 1920s, there were innovations in many areas, such as in art, architecture and education. Maria Montessori founded a school in Italy based on the desire of children to self-develop, they were allowed to choose from the prepared Montessori materials. Peter

Pedersen started his Jenaplan schools, where children could work together on projects and there were no year classes. In Germany, Rudolf Steiner started his education movement based on anthroposophy and Alexander Sutherland Neill (known as A.S. Neill) founded the democratic school Summerhill in 1921 in England. In the Netherlands, Kees Boeke started The Workplace in his house in 1926.

What all these schools have in common is that they take children seriously and they worked on the basis of a more free pedagogy, which allows children themselves to make choices. Many of these innovations were contested by the establishment. The main opponents were and still are the governments, because the governments have, as did the Prussian dictators, given themselves a central role in education. The ruling elites used and still use education mainly as a way to achieve their own objectives, rather than to serve the development of children[95]. A well-known example is that of the Dutch King Willem I, who wanted to use education to forge a unity of the Northern and Southern Netherlands, which were combined after the rule of Napoleon. His initiative was not very well received in the south and was one of the reasons for the Belgian uprising in 1830. This is of all times. The Guardian newspaper headline

---

[95] Glenn, C.L. (2012) State and schools: An historical overview, in: Balancing Freedom, Autonomy and Accountability in Education, Eds. Glenn, C. & Groof, J., Wolf Publishers, Nijmegen. 3-24

on August 17, 2015 was *'Rebel-held Ukraine overhauls education system as it aligns itself with Russia'*[96].

From the perspective of the central role of the government, education faces similar problems as religion. The Pilgrim Fathers were a group of English Protestants who opposed the Anglican Church in the seventeenth century, and as a result they had an immediate problem with the English king, who was the head of the Church of England. This problem was so substantial that a group decided to flee to the Americas and laid the foundation of what is now the USA. The same happened with the Protestants in the Netherlands during the Reformation. They were in conflict with the Roman Catholic Church and therefore immediately had a problem with the Spanish Catholic Kings Charles V and his successor Philip II. This resulted in the establishment of the Republic of the Netherlands, after eighty years of war.

Most education innovators were not as successful as the Dutch Republic or the Pilgrim Fathers. Leo Tolstoy was intimidated by the secret police of the Czar and had to close his school[97]. Maria Montessori had to flee Italy because of her ideas on education and settled in the Netherlands. Peter Petersen was fired from the school where he worked and Rudolf Steiner was opposed by right-wing extremists who later seized the power in Germany.

---

[96] Rebel-held Ukraine overhauls education system as it aligns itself with Russia (2015): www.theguardian.com
[97] Leo_Tolstoy: en.wikipedia.org

After the Second World War, all countries agreed that this horror should never happen again and in 1948 the United Nations adopted the Universal Declaration of Human Rights. These rights were further elaborated in subsequent treaties, including the European Convention of Human Rights and the International Convention on the Rights of the Child. The right to education and rights in education are one of the key rights of children.

Many countries started to build and expand their welfare states after 1945. One of the consequences of building a welfare state was an enormous increase in the number of laws and regulations. This also had its effect on the education sector, were governments already had a great deal of influence. This had two causes. Due to rapidly growing legislation and sprawling bureaucracy the state had more and more influence and control in education. The rationale was that more rules improve quality. The state also emerged as the caretaker of human rights and increasingly saw itself as having (sole) responsibility over the right to education.

In this context many governments regard any fundamental innovation in education as a potential risk to the education of children.

This seems logical and reasonable, but in fact it isn't. Professor Rob Martens (2014) of the Open University in the Netherlands noted during a hearing of the Education

Committee of Parliament that *'The biggest educational experiment of the last hundred years is the experiment that we now call mainstream education. After years of research I have not ben able to find a scientific basis for mainstream education.'* There is no scientific basis for coercive education, with its standardised teaching methods, a standardised curriculum and standardised teachers.

THE BIGGEST EDUCATIONAL EXPERIMENT OF THE LAST 100 YEARS IS THE EXPERIMENT THAT WE NOW CALL MAINSTREAM EDUCATION

- ROB MARTENS

The current educational system is so common now, that almost no one questions the system itself. The system has become a tradition and critical questions are no longer asked. The educational innovator Sugata Mitra has a very critical view of the education system and even says *'The educational system is not broken, it is doing exactly what it has been designed for.... to create people for the bureaucratic administrative machine'*[98].

The human species has been able to cope and develop for the past 100,000 years without mass education. Some of the

---

[98] Sugata, M., (2013), TED talk Build a School in the Cloud: www.youtube.com

greatest massacres and wars have occurred in the 20th century and one of the countries that has played a central role in this also invented the Prussian education system. When children in school are trained to perfection to obey, the step towards the creation of docile, obedient citizens might not be so great. Were human rights and children's rights not created to prevent this? Is it not the duty of every modern democratic state to guard against forcing citizens into a straitjacket?

The risks of experiments in education should also not be judged in absolute terms but in relative terms and be compared to the risks of traditional education. The risks of traditional education are substantial. Students have:

➢ 10% chance of being bullied,
➢ 10% chance of being functionally illiterate,
➢ 15% chance of being prescribed Ritalin or other psychotropic drugs.

The risks of burnout, caused by either stress or chronic boredom, depression, suicide, murder, disease and underachievement are substantial[99]. Children are also coerced to spend some twelve of the most formative and defining years of their lives as prisoners in a school[100]. In comparison the risks of experimental schools are very small: it is virtually impossible for a school to be even worse.

---

[99] Mooij, T., (2014), Onderpresteren van cognitief hoogbegaafde leerlingen in regulier onderwijs: nivoz.nl
[100] Gray, P., School is a Prison! Dr Peter Gray Interviewed on Freedomain Radio, www.youtube.com

Scientific evidence and nearly a century of experience with other forms of education are apparently insufficient for people to believe that things can be done differently, however limiting experiments with other forms of education prevents innovation and thus limits the quality and diversity of educational opportunities, and keeps education stuck in the educational stone age. Without experimentation, innovation is impossible. Imagine that the government had imposed the same policies in other areas - we would drive around in T-Fords, use rotary dial telephones and obtain our wisdom from encyclopaedias. When sick, doctors would still apply blood-letting.

Prohibiting experiments limits the quality of education and is thus infringing the right of children to develop. This is a violation of the rights of the child.

Myth 11 - Bullying is inevitable

Bullying is a common phenomenon in schools. The Saqi website calls bullying a serious epidemic which involves three-quarters of school children[101]. Bullying is one of the central themes of the Children Monitor 2013 of the Dutch National Children's Ombudsman. According to the ombudsman one in ten children is bullied[102]. He defines bullying as systematic and enduring aggression with the aim of causing physical or psychological harm[103].

But this is not the whole story. Despite all the efforts by the government, schools and teachers to prevent and combat bullying, this violence is increasing. The ombudsman presented an overview of types of violence to which children are exposed in schools (see table 1).

The amounts of 'incidental' aggression are much higher than the 10% of children who are bullied, according to the ombudsman. Bullying can have catastrophic effects. Not only can the academic performance of bullied children suffer, but also their welfare and health. This can result in a sense of

---

[101] Pestcijfers: www.saqi.nl
[102] Kinderrechtenmonitor (2013): www.dekinderombudsman.nl
[103] Bullying is defined as a one or more persons trying to inflict systemically psychological or physical damage on another person. There is always a misbalance of power. A relatively new form of bullying is digital bullying. www.nji.nl

insecurity, low self-esteem, low self-belief and it can make the lives of bullied child a kind of hell. In some cases bullying leads to suicide.

	2010	2012
Verbal violence	17%	26%
Material violence	20%	25%
Social violence	20%	23%
Light physical violence	18%	23%
Substantial physical violence	20%	21%

Tabel 1: Percentage of secondary education students who are victims of different types of violence. Source: Social Security Monitor (2012).

The Supreme Court of Mexico stated in a verdict that (2015): *'Bullying is a widespread social phenomenon, very present in Mexican schools and can cause serious harm to the welfare of a minor.'* The school in question was convicted and fined 500,000 pesos (38,000 euros) for bullying[104]. The effects of bullying are not confined to the period when children are at school. The consequences can manifest themselves seriously later in life[105].

Given the seriousness of the matter, it is justified that much is done to protect children against bullying; schools have anti-bullying protocols, anti-bullying methods are

---

[104] Mexico Daily News (2015) School, teacher fined for bullying 7-year-old: http://mexiconewsdaily.com/news/school-teacher-fined-for-bullying-7-year-old/
[105] Kirsten Olsen (2009) Wounded by school, Teachers College Press.

developed, there are anti-bullying courses and statistics are kept. If serious abuses become public, discussions are held in parliament and with the Minister of Education. In the Netherlands, this resulted in 2013 in a law, which requires schools to take action against bullying. This is of course necessary. Because children are forced to go to school, schools must ensure that children are safe while there, however the question is not whether these actions are justified (they certainly are), but whether these actions are effective!

All these actions are taken within the coercive education system. The coercive education system itself is never questioned.

One thing is very clear when the causes of bullying are investigated. Bullying always correlates with power inequality. This is not only the case in schools, but also in other places like companies[106] or government institutions[107] and particularly in prisons and armies. Within any group of the powerless, and so those who are subservient to

---

[106] In bedrijven wordt circa 16% van de werknemers gepest of geïntimideerd: http://conferentieoverpesten.nl/
[107] De zelfmoord van NZa-klokkenluider Arthur Gotlieb heeft pesten op het werk weer onder de aandacht gebracht. Weggetreiterd door de baas (NRC 19 april 2014).

authority, there are often individuals who try to improve their position or to survive, at the expense of others in this group. Bullying is an effective way to gain more power. This results in the creation of a 'pecking order', where a leader arises and around them a group of supporters gathers who try to improve their own position by supporting the leader. If you watch an episode of one of the 'Locked-up' television series, you can see how this works.

The presence of an (uncontrolled) authority in an organisation automatically means that there is a power imbalance. In such a situation bullying can continue for very long periods. A person who is bullied has no means of power to stop the bullying. The only options are to oppose the bullying, or to report the bully to the authority. The effect of the first is usually that the bullying gets worse. The group often sees the second as betrayal, also with the consequence that the bullying worsens. If the authority supports the power imbalance within the group, the threat gets even worse. An option that is rarely mentioned, to move away from the bully, is no longer an option where the victim is trapped, either in prison or in school.

As said, all anti-bullying measures, such as anti-bullying protocols and assertiveness training are undertaken within the education system itself; therefore these measures do not change the system itself. Given that there is a very strong correlation between inequality and bullying it is surprising that almost nobody looks at the coercive education system itself. The coercive system, by definition, creates an authority and a group of powerless people. The whole system consists of a government that suppresses school boards, school boards that suppress teachers and teachers who suppress children[108].

---

[108] Hannam, D., (2015), Lecture at the Conference for Alternative Education Spain.

Similar problems of power imbalance can occur at national level. In a dictatorship, the population has to endure considerable hardship and often suffers from physical and psychological violence. If this violence is serious enough, there is a chance that the population will no longer accept this and rebel. We all know the examples of the French Revolution, the American Revolution, the Dutch Uprising (the Eighty Years' War) and the fall of the Berlin Wall.

In education children in most countries have been stuck for more than one hundred years in an authoritarian system, which is based on the Prussian dictatorship. Within this system approximately 10% of children are bullied. Following the example of the democratic governance of countries, over the last 90 years a small group of schools set themselves up as democratically governed schools. In these schools the children are part of the governance of the school and have equal power, so there is no power inequality and therefore there is also no bullying. This does not imply that incidents do not occur, but if something happens, the children have the power and the means to protect their own safety and the safety of their community as a whole.

If the power imbalance in schools were to be removed, bullying would soon become a thing of the past. As schools themselves have very limited liability to prevent bullying between children[109], governments have an important role here. Governments force children to go to school and most governments subsidise schools 100%. This gives governments a heavy responsibility.

In 2014 the Dutch government funded compulsory education with more than 16 billion euros, to provide education to about 2.4 million students. To put it bluntly, this is 16 billion euro to support institutions where more than 240,000 children are bullied annually and between 500,000 and 600,000 children are exposed to violence (see Table 1).

AUTHORITARIAN SYSTEMS IN SCHOOL REINFORCE BULLYING

Radical but effective ways to stop bullying may be where the government would stop funding schools where children are bullied, or if the government stopped forcing children to go to schools where they are bullied. Another interesting method to combat bullying is practiced in Norway. Here, children who are bullied can report this to their student organisation, which will refer the matter to the school principal. If the principal does not take effective action to stop the bullying, he can be sentenced to a two years in prison[110].

---

[109] Basisboek onderwijsrecht, onder redactie van Prof. Mr. P. W. A. Huisman, p 144.
[110] Hannam, D., 'Another school is possible' (in prep.)

To return to the myth that bullying is inevitable: this is indeed a myth. Schools with their authoritarian systems, despite all good intentions, reinforce bullying. Bullying is a major violation of right of the child to be treated with respect and to be free from physical and psychological violence.

HOW THE EDUCATION SYSTEM REINFORCES ITSELF

This book is not the first to criticise the coercive education system and neither is it the first call for a change of the system. Many have done so before me; Maria Montessori, Leo Tolstoy, Rudolf Steiner, Alexander Sutherland Neill (A.S. Neill), Kees Boeke, Winston Churchill, Albert Einstein, Mark Twain and in current times Daniel Greenberg, Ken Robinson, Sugata Mitra and Claire Boonstra. The question is: why has so little changed? Why do we cling so desperately to the Western tradition of education? A closer look at the education system itself can provide us with insight here.

Forces that strengthen the educational system

Coercive education is the dominant type of education in most countries. Education laws make this system a virtual monopoly. This makes the system itself very attractive for economic and political interest groups (advisory, educational services, suppliers of educational materials and

99

political parties, etc.) so as to safeguard or expand their interests. Through lobbying and political influence, they try to influence the system in a way that is favourable to them. Ultimately, this leads to more legislation and consequently to an increase in the influence of the education system. This makes the system even more attractive for pursuing economic and political goals.

This is a reinforcing vicious circle. For example, as a result of the government decision to provide the expensive schoolbooks for free to students and parents, the publishing companies were relieved of 4 to 5 million discerning customers, they now only need to negotiate with schools, who have little incentive to get the best price as the government pays the bills. Similarly the obligatory tests in primary education provide the Central Institute for Test Development (CITO) with years of employment. The system also has, even without expanding the laws, substantial influence on the thoughts and actions of people. Through the 'phantom legislation' of the Dijsselbloem commission schools adhere to non-existent laws. Another example are the officials of youth care, who wanted to coerce Laura Dekker, even in international waters, to comply with the territorial Compulsory School Act.

Over one hundred years of coercive education has conditioned five generations of citizens to believe that 'coercive education' is normal. When there are problems in education the reaction is 'more education is better' (Myth

1#), which results in pressure to expand in the system. This is a self-reinforcing circle.

Forces that want to change education

Many parents and children see the limitations of the system and want more freedom and alternatives. This creates pressure on the system to allow alternatives and adjust the legislation. Allowing alternatives to the system reduces the influence of the system and thereby threatens the vested interests.

OVER 100 YEARS OF COERCIVE EDUCATION HAS CONDITIONED FIVE GENERATIONS OF CITIZENS TO BELIEF THAT 'COERCIVE EDUCATION' IS NORMAL

How the whole education system strengthens itself

If the system is viewed in its totality it can been seen that the forces, which strengthen the system are institutional forces (the economic and political interests), and forces that change the system, are incidental and not organised (parents and children). Few parents are still committed to changing the system after their children have left school. So as long as there are no substantial opposing forces, the system will only be strengthened. Over the last 100 years, changes in the system have occurred only in small steps, which are so small that they do not create any outrage; 'the boiled frog syndrome'[111,112]. In the Netherlands, many hundred thousands of people demonstrating in The Hague, or large-scale protests by high school students did not have an impact.

The only protection against the uncontrolled expansion of the education system is the constitutional safeguard for freedom of education, but hardly any constitution has been able to stem the tide against the growing influence of the education system on the personal lives of citizens. As Alex Brenninkmeijer, the former National Ombudsman said: *'The Constitution is dead as a mutton'*[113].

DO WE CONTROL THE SYSTEM, OR DOES THE SYSTEM CONROL US?

---

[111] Senge, P.,1990, The Fifth Discipline, The Art & Practice of The Learning Organization, Doubleday.

[112] The boiling frog is an anecdote describing a frog slowly being boiled alive. The premise is that if a frog is put suddenly into boiling water, it will jump out, but if it is put in cold water which is then brought to a boil slowly, it will not perceive the danger and will be cooked to death. The story is often used as a metaphor for the inability or unwillingness of people to react to or be aware of threats that rise gradually.

[113] Brenninkmeijer, A., (2015), Oratie Institutionele aspecten van de rechtsstaat aan de Universiteit Utrecht: www.mr-online.nl

Now the education system is so dominant, and without any serious opposing forces will become even more dominant, that the question is: do we control the system, or does the system control us?

THE HANGOVER AFTER THE EDUCATION PARTY

Where did more than a hundred years of coercive education get us? Over the past century, governments have increasingly prescribed, in detail, the what, how and when in coercive education. The question is whether this was beneficial. In the case of coercive education the end cannot justify the means. Both teachers and MPs have many good intentions, however, education must never be judged on its good

> COERCIVE EDUCATION IS A MAJOR BREACH OF CHILDREN'S FUTURE OPPORTUNITIES

intentions, but only on its results[114]. As the myths show, coercive education does great harm to children and parents. Their freedom and rights are violated on a large scale.

---

[114] Free translated after Milton Friedman: 'One of the great mistakes is to judge policies and programmes by their intentions rather than their results.'

Coercive education often affects the future chances of children, at taxpayers' expense. This not only means that anyone who pays tax is a victim, but is also partly responsible for this and the costs have been rising over years, and in the Netherlands are now at nearly 16 billion euros per year. The justification is that coercive education is in the best interests of children and is needed to create prosperity in the knowledge society. Virtually no politician, from the left or the right, wants less spent on education. Of course you cannot economise on children.

Many children show that coercive education is not their choice. Because they are forced to go to school, they can only express their dissatisfaction at the school. Some do this by rebelling, doing nothing, arrive late or not at all, or talking in class. Others have trouble sitting still for prolonged periods because they find the lessons or the information in the textbooks totally uninteresting.

This type of resistance to compulsory education by children, or rather against coercive education, is initially combatted by disciplinary action by the school and through special needs labels. These labels often lead to medication. If disciplinary measures do not work, the municipal attendance officer takes action, or even the police.

Some parents keep their children at home because they are sick as a result of school or because they are being bullied.

Parents who do not send their children to an approved coercive school often run into problems with attendance officers, possibly followed by (criminal) prosecution. Some parents even end up in the web of youth care services and run the risk of losing parental authority.

In short, schools and the government in the Netherlands harshly oppress all opposition to the coercive education system. This is the same government that, in its wisdom, has decided that only the government can determine what coercive education should look like. This government apparently believes it is better positioned to determine what is good for children than the children and their parents themselves.

But if coercive education is indeed what is best for our children, why is education coercive?

If school were the epitome of learning, children would probably enjoy attending. Why is coercion needed? Why are there so many children who are energetic, curious, interested and only focussed and able to concentrate during the summertime?

> WHY DO MANY CHILDREN SUFFER FROM ABDOMINAL PAIN, HEADACHES OR DEPRESSION WHEN THEY HAVE TO GO TO SCHOOL?

Why do many children suffer from abdominal pain, headaches, or depression when they have to go back to school? Why are there children who vomit every day before they go to school and why don't they have this problem at weekends?

With what purpose was coercive education introduced in 1902? In 1900, when many children were still home-schooled, 90% of children went to a school founded by parents or teachers. These schools were chosen by the parents and children themselves, there was no need for coercion and for children who, for whatever reason, could not go to these private schools, there were public schools set up and run by the government.

John Taylor Gatto shows what coercive education indeed does very effectively in his books. He was a teacher in disadvantaged neighbourhoods in New York, USA, for more than thirty years. He was elected Teacher of the Year for New York City for three consecutive years and Teacher of the Year for New York State. When accepting the last award he announced he had stopped teaching. In his farewell speech, he cited the following reasons: *'Compulsory education teaches confusion, class consciousness, indifference, emotional dependency, intellectual dependence and conditional confidence'*[115]. These are the elements of the

---

[115] Gatto, J.T. (1992), Dumbing Us Down, the Hidden Curriculum of Compulsory Schooling, New Society Publishers.

Prussian education system, which focused on creating loyal and submissive citizens, bureaucrats and soldiers. In such an environment critical thinking is a mortal sin, but critical thinking may be one of the most important, if not the most important skills for children to be successful in the 21st century.

Coercive education also is a major infringement on family life and the leisure of children. A young woman aged thirteen, who wanted to sail around the world was systematically opposed. The parents of the two 'sailing brothers' who could not find a school to accept their children, were prosecuted and initially even deprived of parental authority by the court[116]. A father who found a suitable school for his son, who had crashed in the mainstream education system, ended up in the Kafkaesque world of a government that was acting unlawfully. Parents who were prosecuted and who, due to their great perseverance, were acquitted by a court, did not even receive an apology from the government[117].

There are of course alternatives. Laura Dekker proved she could do well without a diploma. Research shows that children who are home educated are about three years ahead in academic achievement compared to their

---

[116] Geen ondertoezichtstelling voor zeilbroers (2013): www.rechtspraak.nl
[117] Haenen, J., (2014), Van vernieuwer naar verdachte, over innovatief onderwijs en onderwijsvrijheid in Nederland.

counterparts in the traditional education system. Moreover, these home-educated children also appear to outpace their counterparts in social development[118]. Children from democratic schools do well in further education and are allowed into universities. Recently, an alumnus of the Sudbury Valley School won an Oscar for the documentary *Citizen 4* about Edward Snowden[119,120]. Students of democratic schools who return to mainstream education do very well.

The way to improve education is not through more coercion and control, but less. Imposing a system on our children that prepares them for the past is by definition harmful, especially in times where change is accelerating, however this is exactly what governments continue to do. The quality of education can only improve if governments stop interfering with the curriculum and how, when and where our children learn. This requires more freedom for schools!!

In the next chapter I will show the effects of more freedom and of children having more influence on their own education.

---

[118] Blok, H., (2002), 'De effectiviteit van Thuisonderwijs: Een overzicht van onderwijs resultaten', Nederlands Tijdschrift voor Onderwijsrecht en Onderwijsbeleid, 2002, jaargang 14, nr. 4, p. 151-163.]

[119] Poitras, L., (2015), Citizen 4, about the revelations of Edward Snowden.

[120] Laura Poitras: en.wikipedia.org

EXAMPLES OF A DIFFERENT APPROACH

Abolishing coercion in education does NOT mean the abolition of learning. On the contrary, abolishing coercion creates space for schools so they can become temples of learning. Under these circumstances teachers can act on their professional expertise. On top of that, many more alternatives to mainstream education system can be developed. As a former Minister of Education in the Netherlands said, *'Let a thousand flowers blossom'*. Other schools will emerge next to traditional schools that fulfil the needs of particular groups of children and parents. All children will be able to learn in ways that suit them. This means that children will finally be able to fully enjoy their **'right to education'** and **'rights in education'**. It will provide institutions of higher education with the opportunity to select students based on their capacity and motivation, even if they do not have a formal qualification.

'The future is already here - it's just not very evenly distributed' [121] is also true for education. There are already tiny pockets in the world where things happen that are new to most countries. A few examples follow.

Education in Finland[122]

Finland considers good education to be crucial and made a strategic decision in the 1970s; education must focus on learning and not on control. The starting point was thus trust in schools and the professionals who work there. Finland has no school inspection, no national testing or national monitoring of learning results and no school rankings. Schools are flexible in the range of subjects and teaching they provide, and the emphasis is on the broad development of all aspects of individual growth: personality, morality, creativity, knowledge and skills. There are many competent people available as professionals in education, because everyone with a university degree is allowed to teach so long as they obtain a master's degree. For working with younger children the master's degrees should be in an area such as child development, and for older students it should be in the teacher's specialist subject. Teachers are autonomous in how they perform their work. Next to that,

---

[121] William Gibson in Gladstone, (1999).
[122] Sahlberg, P., Ph.D., Director General at Ministry of Education of Finland, (2011), Lecture at Vanderbilt university, Finnish lessons, what can the US learn from educational change in Finland? www.youtube.com

the rights of the child with respect to testing are taken seriously; coercive high stakes testing is not allowed. The testing of students younger than eight years old is prohibited and children under sixteen are only allowed to take a test if they consent. The result of this approach is not only that Finland has scored highly in the PISA comparisons over the last years, but also that education in Finland is much cheaper. The number of contact hours in schools is much lower, teachers can work as professionals, children only have to go to school as from age seven, children have fewer lessons and almost no homework. It seems the Finns are doing something right and many educational experts and professionals visit Finland to learn from their experience. Unfortunately, education laws make it impossible to apply the Finnish model in many countries, including the Netherlands.

Democratic schools

A.S. Neil started Summerhill School in England in 1921[123]. This school has worked for more than ninety years on the basis of personal responsibility for the students and the absence of coercion in learning[124]. The students can choose for themselves whether they attend classes. The school community decides in democratic meetings about the school rules and the enforcement of these rules. The school has

---

[123] Summerhill School, www.summerhillschool.co.uk
[124] Neil, A.S.,(1960), Summerhill School, a new view of childhood, St. Martin's Griffin.

proven itself and alumni have successfully found their way in life[125]. A study in 2000 showed that the results of the final tests were above the national average[126,127].

A group of people in Massachusetts, USA, took the pedagogical concept of Summerhill even further and established the Sudbury Valley School in 1968[128]. The Sudbury Valley School gives students not only responsibility for themselves, but also responsibility for the management of the school. This includes the hiring of staff and taking care of the finances[129]. This school also functions very well. Research into the lives of former students show that they attended the higher education of their choice, found jobs that suited them and led a satisfactory social life. More than 80% of the alumni attended further education, including top universities[130]. Today there are more than fifty Sudbury schools in the world.

In addition to these examples, there are many schools where students have influence in or control over their own

---

[125] Lucas, H. (2011) After Summerhill: What Happened to the Pupils of Britain's Most Radical School? Pomegranate Books.
[126] Cunningham, I., Chairman, Centre for Self Managed Learning (2000), Report of an inquiry into Summerhill school-Leiston, Suffolk , www.selfmanagedlearning.org
[127] East, J., (2008) Summerhill documentary, www.youtube.com
[128] Sudbury Valley School, Framingham, Massachusetts, USA, www.sudval.org
[129] Greenberg,D., et al, (1987), Free at Last, Sudbury valley School Press
[130] Greenberg,D., (2005), The Pursuit of Happiness- the lives of Sudbury Valley Alumni, Sudbury Valley School Press

learning environment through a school community decision-making model. These democratic schools are a rapidly growing phenomenon. There are now more than 280 democratic schools worldwide[131]. In Europe, the European Democratic Education Community (EUDEC) was founded in 2007[132], with the aim *'to promote democratic schools as a sensible educational model for democratic countries'*.

However proven and established Summerhill school and the Sudbury Valley School are, it is not possible to use their pedagogical models in most countries in the world due to national education laws. State funding for these types of schools is often even more difficult as a consequence of stringent funding criteria. In many countries education law forces democratic schools to water down their pedagogical vision and to incorporate elements of mainstream education into their school models in order to be approved by the authorities.

Home-education

Home-education is education at home, often provided by parents. The term 'home education' only determines the location where children learn. The pedagogies of home-educators vary over a broad spectrum, ranging from school at home, with a school bell, curriculum and tests, to un-

---

[131] Democratic schools: www.educationrevolution.org
[132] European Democratic Education Community: www.eudec.org

schooling. 'Un-schooling' is a form of education where the parents are fully confident that their children will learn through their everyday experiences and following their own interests both at home and in the wider community[133]. In the 1970s, home education became the single biggest educational innovation in the US. Some 2-3 million children in the US are home educated. In many countries, home education is now well established as an accepted form of education, and booming. The effects of home education have been intensely researched. This research shows that home education works very well; not only for academic development, but also for social and emotional development[134]. Many universities in the USA are happy to enrol home-educated students, even if they don't have a diploma. Alan Thomas carried out the first detailed study of the methods used in home educating families, based on the interviews and observations of 100 families in Australia and England. The main findings were that nearly every family became less formal over time, with some becoming completely informal and autonomous[135]. Alan and his colleague, Harriet Pattison later embarked on a follow up in-depth study to explore, with parents, how children could

---

[133] C. Bellar (2014) Etre et Devenir (Being and Becoming) http://www.etreetdevenir.com/

[134] Blok, H., (2002), De effectiviteit van thuisonderwijs: Een overzicht van onderzoeksresultaten, Nederlands Tijdschrift voor Onderwijsrecht en Onderwijsbeleid, 2002, jaargang 14, nr. 4, p. 151-163.

[135] Thomas, A. (1998) Educating Children at Home, London, Cassell.

learn so much without being taught. Of particular interest is that many parents, having started out with school type methods, discover autonomous learning for themselves, something that most mainstream educators refuse to acknowledge.

In the Netherlands, home education, which used to be such an accepted form of education that the lawmakers considered it unnecessary to safeguard it in the Constitution, is now virtually impossible. The same situation exists in Germany where it is also not allowed. In many other European countries where home schooling is allowed, governments increasingly try to control it via a mandatory curriculum, coercive testing and inspections.

Self-Learning

Education innovator Sugata Mitra has shown with his *The Hole in the Wall Computer'* experiment, that children are capable of teaching themselves. He performed an experiment in which he placed a computer with an internet connection in the sidewall of a building in a poor neighbourhood in India and observed what happened. It turned out that within a few weeks, the children, who did not speak English, could do anything with the computer; almost to changing the source code. On the basis of several of types of these experiments with 'The Hole in the Wall Computer' he concluded[136]:

- *'Groups of children can learn to use computers and the internet on their own, irrespective of who or where they are'.*

- *'Group self-instruction is as effective as traditional classroom instruction. Such learning is considerably less expensive and independent of teachers and schools'.*

Mitra continued his experiments and showed that children can learn almost everything themselves. He concludes that it is especially important not to stand in the way of learning. Peter Gray, the Author of *'Free to learn'* and research professor of Boston College, concludes exactly the same in his article *'Children's Natural Ways of Educating Themselves Still Work: Even for the Three Rs'*[137]. In most countries 'self-learning' is impossible due to education legislation involving mandatory curricula and coercive testing.

The power of student organisations in Norway

In Norway, school organisations are, along with those of teachers and parents, automatically consulted on proposed changes to the curriculum. School student organisation EON

---

[136] Mitra, S. et al., (2000), Acquisition of computing literacy on shared public computers; Children and the 'hole in the wall'
[137] Gray, P., (2016), Children's Natural Ways of Educating Themselves Still Work: Even for the Three Rs. In: Evolutionary Perspectives on Child Development and Education, Eds. Geary,D. C., Berch D.B., Springer International Publishing part I 67-93

lobbied successfully for more effective anti-bullying legislation. Under Norwegian law, school principals can be penalised by up to two years in prison if they fail to take effective action against bullying once the bullying has been formally reported to them[138]. In most countries, students are powerless and cannot participate in any decision-making concerning their education and their schools. They have virtually no effective means to protect themselves from bullying.

---

[138] Hannam, D., (2015), Lecture at Conference of Alternative Education Spain

THE WAY FORWARD

Many problems in compulsory education, as described in this book, can be traced back to the coercion of children within schools. In addition to the fact that this coercion causes many problems for children, the coercion itself is a direct violation of the rights of the child. The International Convention for the Protection of Human Rights and the Convention on the Rights of the Child should provide the most effective protection against coercion in schools. Most countries ratified the Convention on the Rights of the Child between 1990 and 1995. With the ratification it became mandatory for these governments to realise and actively protect these rights. This convention is an essential part of the liberal constitutional democracy in many countries, including the Netherlands. The convention does not lack clarity, for example, Article 19 for the protection against child abuse, reads:

    1. *'States Parties shall take all appropriate legislative, administrative, social and educational measures to protect the child from all forms of physical or mental violence, injury or abuse, neglect or negligent*

121

treatment, maltreatment or exploitation, including sexual abuse, while in the care of parent(s), legal guardian(s) or any other person who has the care of the child'.

2. *'Such protective measures should, as appropriate, include effective procedures for the establishment of social programmes to provide necessary support for the child and for those who have the care of the child, as well as for other forms of prevention and for identification, reporting, referral, investigation, treatment and follow-up of instances of child maltreatment described heretofore, and, as appropriate, for judicial involvement'.*

This article has been adopted in many countries. These countries have laws that prohibit physical violence against children and governments are actively taking measures to stop physical violence. This is not yet happening in all (European) countries. The Council of Europe reprimanded Belgium in 2015, because the prohibition against physical violence was not yet enshrined in law[139]. It is safe to say that it is now widely accepted that physical violence against children is not allowed, however, what is not universally accepted is the need to guarantee the rights of the child within the schools. The myths described in this book show that within schools, the rights of many children are violated.

---

[139] Belga, (2015), Raad van Europa: 'België is te tolerant voor lijfstraffen voor kinderen, Het Nieuwsblad 29-05-2015: www.nieuwsblad.be

Below I list a few children's rights, which apply under all circumstances - including at school - to each individual child. I will show what it would take to realise these rights in education.

Article 2 (Non-discrimination): The Convention applies to each child, without exception ... (→ *All rights of the child must explicitly be applied, under al circumstances, also within schools. This is not a choice, but something the signatory countries have committed themselves to*).

Article 3 (Best interests of the child): The best interests of children must be the primary concern in making decisions that may affect them... (→ *So no measures may harm the interest of any individual child. The primary concern is the individual interest of any child. Any measures that consider other interests at the expense of individual interests of a child are forbidden*).

Article 4 (Protection of rights): Governments have a responsibility to take all available measures to make sure children's rights are respected, protected and fulfilled... (→ *All necessary measures implies that measures must be effective, it is not an obligation of effort, but an obligation of results. Governments cannot rest until the problems are resolved. In addition, governments must guarantee the rights to education and in education by law*).

Article 6 (Survival and development): ...Governments should ensure that children survive and develop healthily. (→ *it is important that governments safe guard the right to learn of children, rather than to coerce children to and in schools. Governments must provide the resources and opportunities to develop. The government must not impose any barriers to development and eliminate all barriers from education laws and regulations*).

Article 12 (Respect for the views of the child): When adults are making decisions that affect children, children have the right to say what they think should happen and have their opinions taken into account... (*This gives the child the right to decide on all matters concerning their education. After all, sharing an opinion that is not acted upon is meaningless*).

Article 13 (Freedom of expression): Every child has the right to get and share information... (→ *so each child can give his opinion on any matter it considers relevant, limited only by the prohibition on discrimination and hate speech*).

Article 14: (Freedom of thought, conscience and religion): Every child has the right to freedom of thought, conscience and religion and freedom to express this ... (→ *See article 13*).

Article 15: (Freedom of association): Children have the right to meet together and to join groups and organisations...

124

(→ *This is the right of association and assembly for every child and means that every child must, also in schools, be able to gather with people of different ages at a time that he chooses*).

Article 16: (Right to privacy): Children have a right to privacy... (→ *This means, that schools can only register or discuss information with the prior consent of the child. This also includes the disclosure of test results, the personal information that is stored in student tracking systems and who has access to this personal information*).

Article 19 (Protection from all forms of violence): Children have the right to be protected from being hurt and mistreated, physically or mentally... (→ *This requires effective protection against physical and psychological violence including bullying and having access to effective legal remedies*).

Article 28 (Right to education): Every child has the right to education ... Enforcing discipline in schools must be compatible with human dignity and in conformity with the Convention on the Rights of the Child (→ *This means eliminating arbitrariness in the enforcement discipline, elimination of bullying and applying the principles of the rule of law within the school*).

Article 29 (Goals of education): Children's education should develop each child's personality, talents and abilities to the fullest. It should encourage children to respect others, human rights... (→ *This means that the human rights must also be respected and lived in schools, including the unconstrained right to develop*).

Article 31 (Leisure, play and culture): Children have the right to relax and play, and to join in a wide range of cultural, artistic and other recreational activities... (→ *So even in school every child must have enough free time and the opportunity to play and recreate. This requires the elimination of coercion in schools, schoolwork during breaks, evenings, weekends and holidays, and long school days*).

Article 32 (Child labour): The government should protect children from work that is dangerous or might harm their health or their education. (→ *Schoolwork may therefore not be dangerous, harmful or hinder development. This requires the elimination of stress, coercion, bullying and exposure to hazardous substances, unhealthy air or unhygienic buildings. Coercive testing can slow development*).

Article 33: (Drug abuse): Governments should use all means possible to protect children from the use of harmful drugs.... (→ *Medications used with diagnoses like ADHD are drugs, against which each child must be protected*).

In Conclusion

The rights of the child are regularly violated in virtually all schools. Being bullied is a violation of the rights of the child, as is coercive testing and the restriction of freedom, restriction of movement, prohibition to talk or think freely, having no say in decisions that concern the child, as well as any barriers to development. As I showed earlier, coercive education makes many children sick. Many of these 'diseases' from which children suffer are similar to the 'diseases' that manifested in slaves on plantations; drapetomania (the tendency to flee)[140] or dysaethesia aethiopica (a pathological lack of motivation)[141]. From the perspective of slaveholders these were indeed 'diseases', as slavery was 'normal' at the time, and thus opposition to slavery had to be a 'disease' to be combatted with medication, imprisonment, whipping or amputation. The real problem of the slaves was of course that they were

---

[140] https://en.wikipedia.org/wiki/Drapetomania
[141] https://en.wikipedia.org/wiki/Dysaesthesia_aethiopica

127

slaves and had no freedom to organise their own lives, and had to live and work under coercion. To many people this only became apparent after the abolition of slavery. Women have also long been in a position of dependency and also had their own 'diseases', such as chlorosis, anorexia and hysteria. These disorders had everything to do with a lack of freedom and lack of future prospects. One of the arguments against women's suffrage was that women were like children and therefore could not handle responsibility[142], yet the world did not end with the introduction of women's suffrage!

Unfortunately, even in these days, their basic rights and freedoms are withheld from children. In fact their rights and freedoms are decreasing continuously. Governments continue to take measure after measure to expand their control over education and because governments not only do not trust parents and their children, but also schools and teachers, they continue on the path of more coercion and more control. Abolishing coercion in education will solve many of the problems in schools and this can be achieved through the realisation of the rights of the child within schools.

---

[142] constitutioncenter.org

SLAVES AND WOMEN HAVE ALREADY
REALISED THEIR RIGHTS:

19TH CENTURY: ABOLITION OF SLAVERY!

20TH CENTURY: FREEDOM FOR WOMEN!

21ST CENTURY: FREEDOM FOR CHILDREN ...

Thanks to

I have only been able to gain experience and develop insights for this book thanks to the support and energy of all the people who were involved in the launch of three schools: De Ruimte, De Kampanje and Newschool.nu. In 2003 we started with De Ruimte in Soest; a democratic school modelled after Iederwijs. In 2007 we founded De Kampanje in Amersfoort, a Sudbury model school, and in 2014 the successor to the Kampanje, Newschool.nu. I would like to thank all the founders, staff and students of De Ruimte, De Kampanje and Newschool.nu who took part in this great adventure. In preparing the lawsuits we received legal supported from Rita Vlemminx, Peggy Lesquiller and Jan De Groof, and our own legal club consisting of Anjo Snijders, Jaap Haenen, Michael de Vos and Edwin de Bree. Derry Hannam, Peter Gray, Alan Thomas, Rob Martens and Wim Timmer played an important role as expert witnesses in all the court cases. The litigation itself would not have been possible without the unwavering support of Tom Barkhuyzen and Machteld Claessens, who represented us in the administrative courts, and Muriel Rosing who represented all parents in the criminal courts. Over the years we have received a great deal of support from the Sudbury community, especially from Edwin de Bree of De Koers in Beverwijk, the Netherlands, Rikke Knudsen of Roskilde Sudbury School, Denmark, Maaike Eggermont from the Sudbury School Ghent, Belgium, Monika Wernz and Simone Kosog from the Sudbury Schule Ammersee, Germany, Ricky and Eudice Ben Or and Shoshanna London Sappir of the Jerusalem Sudbury School, Israel and Mimsy Sadofsky, Hannah and Daniel Greenberg of the Sudbury Valley School in Boston, USA, and all the people who contributed to the crowd funding to pay a portion of the costs of the litigation.

We have also kept the Dutch school inspectorate quite busy over the past fifteen years. I want to specially thank the inspectors Kees van Baak and Martin Uunk for making this adventure possible, by disagreeing with us on almost every single point, but with whom we have nevertheless always maintained a good relationship.

For providing comments on this book, I would like to thank the following people: Gerard Chel, Sandra Weerman, Edwin de Bree, Simon Hulshof, Fieke van der Veen, Michael de Vos, Jaap Haenen Simone Haenen, Pim Monquil, Ton and Carol Romein, Hetty Hartkamp, Willemijn Hartkamp, Ada van der Gaag, Patrick Nederkoorn, Toine Manders and Anne Marie Smetsers. For editing the English version I would like to thank Derry Hannam, Alan Thomas, John Moravec, Richard Plenty and Peter Gray.

I also want to express my special thanks to Christel Hartkamp-Bakker for joining me on this great adventure and for her tremendous support, criticism, lengthy discussions and the preparation of this book, and to Liselotte Hartkamp for drawing the cartoons.

About the Author

Peter Hartkamp (1961), after studying mining engineering at the Technical University in Delft and working for a Dutch Petroleum Company, moved in 1994 with his wife and three daughters to the Sultanate of Oman, where the children attended a Dutch primary school. In 1998, the family moved back to the Netherlands. Since then education, education law and human rights has constantly demanded his attention. He has been co-founder and staff member of three schools, including two Sudbury schools. His experience as a strategy consultant helped him with a sharp analysis of education. Peter Hartkamp is also active in the Council of the European Democratic Education Community (EUDEC) and he gives presentations on education and human rights in different countries.

peter@hetgedwongenonderwijsvoorbij.nl

RECOMMENDED BOOKS

Free at Last: The Sudbury Valley School-Daniel Greenberg, Sudbury Valley School Press, 1995, ISBN 978-1888947007

Free to Learn: Why Unleashing the Instinct to Play Will Make Our Children Happier, More Self-Reliant, and Better Students for Life, Peter Gray, Basic Books, 2015, ISBN 978-0465084999

Turning Learning Right Side Up: Putting Education Back on Track, Russel Ackoff and Daniel Greenberg, FT Press, 2008, ISBN 978-0132887632

A Place to Grow: The Culture of Sudbury Valley School, Daniel Greenberg, Sudbury Valley School Press, 2016, ISBN 978-1888947267

Wounded by school, Kirsten Olson, Teachers College Press, 2009, ISBN 978-0807749555

Schools on Trial, Nikhil Goyal, Doubleday, 2016, ISBN 978-0385540124

Case Against Adolescence, Robert Epstein, Quill Driver Books / Word Dancer Press, Inc., 2007, ISBN 978-1884956706

Rethinking Learning to Read, Harriet Pattison, Educational Heretics Press, 2016, ISBN 978-1900219464

Printed in Great Britain
by Amazon

34059914R00085